A Dictionary of Coastal Command 1939–1945

A Dictionary of Coastal Command 1939–1945

Geoff Simpson

Pen & Sword
AVIATION

First published in Great Britain in 2017 by
Pen & Sword Aviation
an imprint of
Pen & Sword Books Ltd
47 Church Street
Barnsley
South Yorkshire
S70 2AS

ISBN 978 1 47387 271 4

A CIP catalogue record for this book is available from the British
Library

Typeset in Ehrhardt by
Mac Style Ltd, Bridlington, East Yorkshire
Printed and bound in the UK by CPI Group (UK) Ltd,
Croydon, CRO 4YY

Pen & Sword Books Ltd incorporates the imprints of Pen & Sword
Archaeology, Atlas, Aviation, Battleground, Discovery, Family
History, History, Maritime, Military, Naval, Politics, Railways,
Select, Transport, True Crime, and Fiction, Frontline Books, Leo
Cooper, Praetorian Press, Seaforth Publishing and Wharncliffe.

For a complete list of Pen & Sword titles please contact
PEN & SWORD BOOKS LIMITED
47 Church Street, Barnsley, South Yorkshire, S70 2AS, England
E-mail: enquiries@pen-and-sword.co.uk
Website: www.pen-and-sword.co.uk

Contents

Author's Note

In general, the ranks attributed to service personnel are the ones in which they were serving at the relevant time. Any attempt to differentiate between the various classes of rank, including substantive, wartime substantive, temporary and acting would probably create considerable confusion. A number of important RAF Coastal Command stations have been given their own entries, as examples of the locations from which the Command operated.

Foreword

"Battles might be won or lost, enterprises might succeed or miscarry, territories might be gained or quitted, but dominating all our power to carry on in the war, or even to keep ourselves alive, lay our mastery of the ocean routes and the free approach and entry to our ports ... the only thing that ever frightened me during the war was the U-boat peril."

Sir Winston Churchill

Advances in technology in the twentieth century meant that military history was littered with examples of the "horse versus tank" moment. Yet, the full implications of these technologically-driven capabilities were rarely obvious at the time. One such example goes to the heart of the history of Coastal Command. On a typical February day in 1935 in a Northamptonshire field, Robert Watson-Watt and his team demonstrated the detection capability of what we now know as radar. It was this invention, plus the eight-gun fighter at the tip of the spear, that subsequently delivered victory in the Battle of Britain. However, it also meant that the RAF's fundamental doctrine, which was also the bedrock upon which the notion of an independent air force rested, that 'the bomber will always get through', was fundamentally flawed. It was this realisation that gave rise to the 1936 reorganisation of the RAF's command structure and saw the creation of Coastal Command alongside Bomber Command and Fighter Command.

From early days, Coastal Command was dubbed the "Cinderella" of the trio. The mainstay was ten squadrons of Ansons which were entirely unsuited to the type of maritime patrol missions which were bound to confront an island nation engaged in a war of national survival. Lessons from the devastating U-boat threat in the First World War were fresh in the memory. Yet, it took until late 1937 before any clarity emerged on the role of Coastal Command with trade protection and co-operation with the Royal Navy then featuring prominently in the script. Clearly, by comparison with Fighter Command and Bomber Command, Coastal Command was therefore not master of its own destiny. Whereas in all cases the enemy would have a vote, the war at sea was seen primarily as the Royal Navy's business. Here lie the beginnings of the rather ambiguous sense of ownership by the RAF for its maritime capability. At the time, this was manifest in the competition for the aircraft industry's industrial capacity, with Coastal Command coming a distant third. More recently, it was reflected in the 2010 decision to scrap the Nimrod MRA4 and with it, an RAF capability that had achieved some seventy years of continuous and, occasionally compelling, operational success. While this significant deficit has now been partially remedied by the decision to acquire the Boeing P-8 Poseidon, the resulting yawning capability gap of some eight years has seen the dissipation of both the tacit knowledge and cultural excellence that were embedded in the DNA of the RAF's maritime force.

In terms of compelling operational success, the Battle of the Atlantic must stand supreme and Churchill's view on the odds was very clear. Whilst this battle waged over four long years, the Command's aircraft were initially incapable of reaching the key hunting grounds of the U-boat wolf-packs and lacked any sensors to enhance the crews' own visual detection capability. Indeed, resources were so tight against the RAF's other priorities that Lord Beaverbrook proposed to the Defence Committee that ownership of Coastal Command should pass to the Royal Navy. The subsequent enquiry disagreed: rather, it emphasised the operational harmony which had been achieved between Coastal Command and the Royal Navy, a facet that was equally apparent throughout the decades that followed. Understanding the catalyst for this unhelpful intervention takes us back to that Northamptonshire field of February 1935. Radar development had come-on apace, and there was now the prospect of an airborne submarine detection radar, then known as ASV 1. While it had a difficult gestation, it was nevertheless a game-changer. By mid-1942, developments had increased the detection range to twelve miles ahead and twenty miles on the beam. In parallel, the development of Leigh Light at last gave the Command a night detection capability.

While both these enhancements were pretty rudimentary in their performance, they provided a stimulus to crews to apply the maximum tactical creativity to increase the odds of a successful attack. Prime amongst such thinkers was Squadron Leader Terry Bullock DSO* DFC* of No. 120 Squadron, the highest-scoring Coastal Command pilot, whose inspirational leadership permeated crews far beyond his own squadron. There was, equally, no shortage of tenacity and courage: Coastal Command aircrew won four VCs. This collective example of determination, professionalism and tactical skill acted as the golden thread through the subsequent history of Coastal Command and its successors. In many ways, this cohesive spirit was generated because of the large crew environment, the relentless grind of long-range maritime aviation and the sheer doggedness to succeed fuelled by constantly feeling under-resourced and under-appreciated, made a major contribution to operational success.

Operational success was a paramount objective too during the Cold War. Every week, Soviet submarines would be on the loose to interdict the West's nuclear deterrent submarines. The Nimrod's ability to track them, gather acoustic intelligence and, if ordered in war, to sink them was a vital element of encouraging caution in the minds of Warsaw pact commanders and in undermining the confidence of the submarine commanders in the Soviet Northern Fleet. Yet none of this was in the public domain until the BBC's 1978 *Panorama* programme revealed the existence of the under-sea listening arrays and the Nimrod's part in the plan. The Tom Clancey novel, *The Hunt for Red October*, did the rest. But, again, the technology then was rudimentary and relied much on the human creativity of the crew; we really did play three-dimensional chess. Similarly, the aircraft's versatility increased with technological advances in sensors and communications seeing it play a compelling role in the Falklands war, two Gulf wars, in the Balkans and in Afghanistan. Deeper in history, "small wars" kept Coastal Command's Shackleton crews equally busy in far-flung places. In all of these endeavours, the human spirit was to predominate but many of us waited in vain for Cinderella's fairy godmother to appear.

This Coastal Command Dictionary compiled by Geoff Simpson with characteristic clarity and forensic attention to detail, adds welcome texture to the received wisdom on Coastal Command's history. It also fills-in a number of gaps on aspects that have not previously been recorded. As both a scholarly reference book and as a highly-digestible narrative, it serves as a justifiable tribute to more than seventy years of the RAF's maritime aviation heritage whose characteristics are accurately reflected in Coastal Command's motto of 'Constant Endeavour'.

Air Chief Marshal Sir Brian Burridge KCB, CBE
Commander-in-Chief Strike Command, 2003–2006

Sir Brian Burridge was commissioned into the Royal Air Force in 1967 as a University Cadet at Manchester University Air Squadron. As a pilot and flying instructor, he served in the Nimrod maritime patrol force with Nos. 206 and 120 Squadrons but with a tour in command of Cambridge University Air Squadron in between. He then commanded the Nimrod Operational Conversion Unit and RAF Kinloss, and was later AOC No. 11/18 Group. Ministry of Defence appointments included three years as Principal Staff Officer to the Chief of the Defence Staff.

Sir Brian commanded the UK Joint Contingent in the Iraq War of 2003 and was Commander-in-Chief, Strike Command from 2003 to 2006.

Introduction

Possibly the first publication on the RAF that I ever read was the HMSO account of Coastal Command's activities in the early years of the war. I don't know why that, and the story of HMS *Ark Royal* of similar style and date, were in the family home sixty years ago, but they left a strong impression.

Writing this book has given me the opportunity to delve much deeper into the "Cinderella Service", as Coastal Command regarded itself, and learn far more about the challenges and the heroism involved in fighting the U-boats, sinking the ships supplying the German war effort and so many other tasks as well, generally carried out over seas which could be hostile and, indeed, cruel.

The part that the Command played in winning the Second World War is not always accorded its full due, perhaps to some extent because its efforts were less obvious than those of Bomber and Fighter Commands and less easily explained by journalists in the limitations of newspaper space. As this book demonstrates, so often too, the achievements of Coastal Command and its development were entwined with the Royal Navy and its operations.

That Coastal Command was at least the equal of other RAF Home Commands in ensuring that Nazism did not triumph is something that should always be remembered.

Geoff Simpson
March 27 2016

Acknowledgements

Many people have shared their knowledge with me over the years and helped to make writing this book a most enjoyable experience. Inevitably, some have not lived to receive these thanks. Those to whom I have reason to be grateful include:

Lady Aitken
Kristen Alexander
Group Captain Tom Barrett, OBE
Colonel Paul Beaver
Gerry Burke
Air Chief Marshal Sir Brian Burridge, KCB, CBE
Deborah Burns
Flight Lieutenant Owen Burns
Simon Butler
Ian Chisholm, Coastal Command and Maritime Air Association
Ian Coleman
Sebastian Cox, Air Historical Branch (RAF)
Philip Curtis
Group Captain Alex Dickson, OBE, QVRM, AE
Fred Dunster
Wing Commander "Tim" Elkington
John Evans. Pembroke Dock Sunderland Trust
Nia Evans
Air Chief Marshal Sir Christopher Foxley-Norris, GCB, DSO, OBE
Group Captain Tom Gleave, CBE

Gary Godel

Didy Grahame, The Victoria Cross and George Cross Association

John Grehan

Terry Hissey

Richard Hunting, CBE

Imperial War Museums

Wing Commander C G Jefford, MBE

Tim Johnson, Online Parish Clerk (Geneology) for St Eval

Michael Korda

Laura Levi

Martin Mace

Edward McManus

National Army Museum

The 2nd Lord Newall, DL

Air Commodore Graham Pitchfork, MBE

Pritzker Military Library

RAF Lossiemouth

RAF Museum

Wing Commander Andy Simpson RAFVR(T)

Margaret Simpson

John Sweeney

Victoria Thompson

The 3rd Viscount Thurso, PC

John Tilley

Group Captain Patrick Tootal, OBE, DL

John White, Australian War Memorial

Kenneth G Wynn

A

Aalesund (or Alesund) – Norwegian port on a number of islands a little less than 150 miles north-north-east of Bergen. British wartime documents often spelt it "Aalesund".

On the night of October 29 1941, Aalesund was attacked by nine Hudsons of No. 220 Squadron, in an operation which the Coastal Command historian, Andrew Hendrie (who flew operationally with the Command in the Second World War), considered the most successful strike ever undertaken by Coastal Command. Accounts vary as to how many ships were put out of action – between two and four – and there were no RAF casualties.

"The reasons for the Hudsons' success," wrote Hendrie, "were due to their crews, which by then had gained much successful experience; they were a small number, all in one squadron, led by their own commanding officer, the raid was in a harbour and they gained surprise."

Aalesund from the air a few hours before the major attack.

At the time the Air Ministry claimed that up to thirty German ships may have been sunk or damaged in less than a week of specialised attacks.

"The harbour and anchorages of the Norwegian port of Aalesund – one of the bases from which Hitler supplies his northern Russian front – were wreathed in smoke and flames for hours last night and this morning following the most devastating shipping attack ever carried out by a single squadron of the RAF." (From a contemporary bulletin issued by the Air Ministry).

"The 'planes flew through snowstorms across the North Sea to unload their bombs on a large concentration of shipping and when they had finished, in the words of one pilot, 'the burning ships outshone the moon,'" (From the report which appeared in the *Glasgow Herald*).

Aerial Minelaying – Mines were laid by the RAF in many areas of European waters during the Second World War, with both Bomber and Coastal Commands engaged in the work. Often the RAF was able to reach areas not accessible to the Royal Navy.

All minelaying was under the control of the Navy, so that there was close inter-service co-operation. For minelaying purposes the European coastline was divided into six areas:-

1. The Western Baltic
2. The Kattegat, Kiel, the Sound and Belts
3. The South Coast of Norway
4. The North Sea; Danish, German and Netherlands coasts
5. The Belgian and northern French coasts
6. The French Biscay coasts

Individual locations in these areas were usually given horticultural code names, such as geranium and lettuce and were referred to as "gardens". Mines were known as "vegetables" and the term "gardening" became commonplace for minelaying.

The start of the campaign was pinpointed in an article in the *RAF Historical Society Journal* (No. 45, 2009) by Air Commodore Graham Pitchfork, in which he wrote, "Hampdens of No 5 Group [Bomber Command] …, each carrying a single mine, carried out the first British aerial minelaying operation on the night of April 13/14 1940 when 13 Mk I magnetic mines were laid in the Great and Little Belts off the Danish coast. The following night Beauforts of Coastal Command, also carrying a mine each, laid six mines off the Ems and Weser rivers. These first aerial minelays coincided with the German occupation of Denmark and Norway."

By the end of 1941 the Coastal Command Beauforts were being utilised almost exclusively in their torpedo bomber guise, leaving the "Gardening" role to Bomber Command (which saw it as a method of crew training), with some assistance from the Fleet Air Arm. The arrival of more heavy bombers during 1942 enabled bomber squadrons to place more mines and Bomber Command took sole responsibility for the task from March of that year.

Air Sea Rescue – Before the Second World War there was little formal provision for rescuing downed aircrew from the sea. The RNLI, of course, did sterling work; there were sometimes RAF high speed launches (HSLs) available and use was made of shipping available in the area. Aerial searches were largely left to the unit that "owned" the missing aircraft. Ahead of the declaration of war it was agreed to make more HSLs available. Responsibility for the co-ordination of searches was given to the various Coastal Command Groups, but the approach to a vital task remained haphazard.

A crisis was reached in the summer of 1940 during Fighter Command operations over the Channel ports and in the Battle of Britain. Many pilots and other aircrew were going into the sea and a significant proportion was not being rescued, at least by the British. This led to some unorthodox rescue attempts. On September 27 1940, for example, off Folkestone, Pilot Officer "Pip" Cardell of No. 603 Squadron jumped from his stricken Spitfire. His parachute failed to open. However, Pilot Officer Keith Dexter, of the same squadron, having failed to attract attention on the shore, crash-landed on the beach, commandeered a rowing boat, but found himself recovering Cardell's body.

Pilot Officer "Tim" Elkington of No. 1 Squadron did not land in the sea after baling out of a burning Hurricane on August 16 1940. Instead Flight Sergeant Frederick Berry used his aircraft to blow Elkington to a landing at West Wittering, Sussex. By chance Elkington had taken to his parachute near the Nab Tower Light, the structure of which was originally part of a planned First World War U-boat defence system consisting of towers and booms. It was far from complete when hostilities ceased.

Flight Sergeant Berry would be lost in action on September 1 1940.

At this point German rescue of their aircrew (and sometimes British as well) was more effective. Their float planes operated close to the English coast, despite RAF pilots being under orders to shoot them down (the Luftwaffe also attacked British aircraft engaged in rescue work). In addition, combat aircraft often carried inflatable rubber dinghies and use was made of a chemical method of causing the sea around an airman to turn bright green. Some aircrew considered the German lifejacket to be superior to the "Mae West".

Improvement had come about from July 1940, when Air Vice-Marshal Park, commanding Fighter Command's No. 11 Group, and working in conjunction with Bertram Ramsay, Vice Admiral, Dover, had obtained some Army Co-operation Lysanders to be used to assist HSLs in searches for downed aircrew. Dye and other equipment improvements were adopted. Lysanders were officially transferred to Fighter Command in August 1940.

Pilot Officer (later Wing Commander) Jack Rose recalled that the dye was issued to No. 32 Squadron pilots on the morning of August

25 1940, with instructions that the pack be sewn on their life jackets. Shortly afterwards at dispersal, Rose performed the task. At about 19.00 hours that day Rose and Pilot Officer Keith "Colt" Gillman were both shot down over the Channel. Two hours later a searching aircraft from the squadron spotted a dye stain and directed a ship to Rose. By Rose's account Gillman had not undertaken the sewing task. He was not found.

In January 1941 a Directorate of Sea Rescue Services was set up at the Air Ministry. Its functions were later taken over by the Directorate of Aircraft Safety. Coastal Command was made responsible for air sea rescue that was required more than twenty miles from the British coast.

The existing Fighter Command rescue units became Nos. 275–278 Squadrons. Two ASR squadrons were formed in Coastal Command – No. 279 at Bircham Newton and No. 280 at Thorney Island. In theory both were equipped with Hudsons, but such was the demand for the type for other duties that No. 280 started with Ansons and some were also operated by No. 279. Flying boats, notably the Walrus and Sunderland, were used to land on the sea to pick up survivors. Fighters were equipped with dinghies. Later the Vickers Warwick was used as an ASR aircraft and became one of the types to drop lifeboats.

Further new equipment was developed. From 1941 the practice was to issue aircrew with whistles for attracting attention after being downed.

A rescue that attracted some attention at the time and later was that carried out on October 22 1941, by a Sunderland of No. 10 Squadron, RAAF, skippered by Flight Lieutenant Reg Burrage, RAAF, flying from Pembroke Dock. The aircraft in trouble was a Whitley attached to No. 502 Squadron at St Eval from No. 612 Squadron at Wick. It was returning on one engine from an anti-submarine patrol off the coast of Spain and the pilot was Pilot Officer D. H. Limbrey.

Burrage later recorded that his aircraft, "Reached the latest recorded position of the Whitley ... and commenced a square search. After completing two legs of the search received a signal from base giving a later estimated position of the Whitley which was further east towards The Lizard, and set course accordingly ... We had almost reached The Lizard when we intercepted a signal from a Hudson (indicating that it was over a dinghy containing five live aircrew) ... Dropped a smoke float near the dinghy and waved as we flew low over the survivors."

Burrage was ordered by base not to land, "unless conditions permit". For some time Burrage reflected on the right course of action to take. There was not much daylight left, the swell was "fairly moderate by Atlantic standards", though difficult to assess and the sea was broken with white caps and appeared to be about eight feet from trough to

An airborne lifeboat is parachuted by a Lockheed Hudson of No. 279 Squadron to the crew of a USAAF Boeing B-17 who had difficulty in getting into their dinghy after making a forced landing in the North Sea on July 26 1943.

crest. Eventually Burrage decided to jettison his bombs and depth charges and try to land. A landing was effected and, after considerable difficulty, the six men in a two-man dinghy were picked up.

Later, the Air Officer Commanding No. 19 Group, Air Vice-Marshal G. R. Bromet signalled, "Well done. You have shown great initiative and fine seamanship. I hope the Whitley crew are none the worse for their experience."

In considering whether to land, Reg Burrage had no doubt taken into account an earlier open sea landing in which he had been involved, as second pilot, where the Sunderland was so badly damaged that it had to be sunk by the Royal Navy after its crew and four RAF survivors had been taken off.

"20 AIRMEN SAVED IN DAY"

The air sea rescue service of a Coastal Command Group rescued 20 airmen yesterday. In addition to nine survivors of a Sunderland, the crew of seven of a four-engine bomber were saved after being in their dinghy for only two-and-a-half hours. A Walrus took them aboard just before a Coastal Command high speed launch arrived. Not one of the seven was injured.

"In the evening the crew of four of another aircraft was rescued."

(From the *Daily Telegraph*, April 17 1943).

Air to Surface Vessel (ASV) – A radar system developed in the run-up to hostilities. Installation of ASV Mk I in Coastal Command aircraft, initially Hudsons and Sunderlands, began early in the war. Improved performance was achieved with the introduction of Long Range ASV and ASV Mk II. It transpired that ASV could detect submarines as well as surface vessels.

There was considerable further development and competition between Coastal Command and Bomber Command for equipment suitable for the purposes of those Commands.

An Aldis lamp being used to signal from an aircraft to a convoy.

Aldis Lamp – A signalling lamp invented by Arthur Aldis which was produced in various sizes. Such lamps were used for signalling from aircraft, often by means of Morse Code.

Altmark – A 12,000 ton German tanker used to supply the pocket battleship, *Admiral Graf Spee*, before it was scuttled in December 1939 after the Battle of the River Plate. In February 1940 the *Altmark* was returning to Germany carrying almost 300 seamen captured by the *Admiral Graf Spee* from British ships.

The British were determined to free these prisoners, but, as the *Altmark* hugged the coast of Norway, then a neutral country, the Royal Navy lost the ship. Coastal Command was tasked to undertake a search and a Hudson of No. 220 Squadron, captained by Pilot Officer C. W. McNeill, located the quarry as it made its way to Jossing Fjord. The diplomatic position was delicate, but the destroyer HMS *Cossack*, with direct intervention by Winston Churchill as First Lord of the Admiralty, was eventually ordered to sail into the fjord and liberate the prisoners. The *Cossack* brushed aside attempts by Norwegian naval vessels to prevent it entering the area and went alongside the *Altmark*.

A boarding party, led by Lieutenant Bradwell Turner, then sought the prisoners and the words, "The Navy's Here", sometimes said to have been shouted by one of the boarding party, entered wartime

The German prison ship *Altmark* photographed in Jossing Fjord, Norway. It is believed to be one of a series of images taken by Flying Officer R. G. M. Walker of No. 224 Squadron, Coastal Command.

folklore. The merchant seamen were returned safely to Britain, though there were casualties amongst the German crew. Reference is often made to "The Altmark Incident".

Anti-Shipping – In the first years of the war Coastal Command attacked enemy shipping with great gallantry, but at a fearful cost.

John Terraine in *The Right of the Line* recorded that, in the last quarter of 1941, the Command sank fifteen hostile ships, while losing forty-six aircraft. In the next quarter the figures were worse – six ships sunk with fifty-five aircraft lost.

Unsurprisingly, this rate of attrition was clearly having an impact on the squadrons. Terraine quoted the war diary of No. 407 Squadron, RCAF, referring to the period in 1942 when it was based at Bircham Newton and flying the Hudson III and then Hudson V – "Since the squadron became operational again on 1st April we have lost twelve crews, in all fifty persons either missing or killed. During the past month six crews have been designated missing or killed on operations with the loss of twenty-seven lives. This does not take into consideration the fact that after every major operation of this nature at least two or three aircraft are so very badly damaged that they are of no use to this, or any other squadron."

Terraine went on to applaud the bravery of men carrying out attacks in which the extremely low level of their assault was sometimes evidenced by the souvenirs of their targets carried by returning aircraft. He attributed losses in part to the despatch of experienced crews to the Middle East and the increasing capability of German anti-aircraft defences. In July 1942 the order came down that low level attacks were to cease. At medium level the success rate declined accordingly.

Minelaying achieved results and the advent of the Strike Wings (see separate entries for Aerial Minelaying and Strike Wings) greatly improved the situation.

"What a sight it was! The whole convoy, which a moment before had been sailing peacefully down the coast was now covered by a pall of smoke." Squadron Leader Jack Davenport, RAAF, describes an attack on a German convoy, just off the coast of southern Norway on July 15 1944. "Ships were on fire and sinking. Everywhere, dozens of aircraft were diving, firing and turning in all directions. As I broke away, I saw the largest vessel in the convoy with a mass of flames from stem to stern. Just in front of it there came a terrific explosion and steam and water spouted up to 300 or 400 feet. When it subsided, the ship that had been there was there no longer. She blew up without leaving a single trace." (Quoted in *Jack Davenport, Beaufighter Leader* by Kristen Alexander).

The sortie involved 44 Beaufighters of Nos. 144, 404, 455 and 489 Squadrons. The convoy consisted of four merchant vessels and five escort ships.

Squadron Leader Phil Evans, DFC (centre), Flying Officer Fox (left) and Flying Officer Smith show off the damage to their No. 59 Squadron Hudson, FH 426, caused by anti-aircraft fire during shipping strikes off the Dutch coast on July 30 1942.

Anti-Submarine – "The first requirement of an Air Force is to have aircraft and Coastal Command, throughout the war, had none that had been designed specifically for anti submarine warfare. In the U-boat war it was the American-built aircraft such as Hudsons, Catalinas and Liberators, that served to a considerable extent and without which the British would have been in dire straits. Notably, the Liberators were able to close the Mid-Atlantic Gap." (Andrew Hendrie in *The Cinderella Service*).

The German Navy began a major submarine campaign immediately on the outbreak of war in September 1939. During August 1939 it had already deployed possibly as many as forty U-boats in the Atlantic in readiness for what was to come. On the evening of September 3, the SS *Athenia* (Donaldson Atlantic), sailing from Glasgow to Montreal, was torpedoed off Rockall by *U-30*. Although the ship remained afloat for a considerable time, there were deaths, including American citizens. The Germans had imposed restrictions on targets to be attacked and the submarine's captain claimed that he had believed the ship to be armed.

The official publication, *A Brief History of the Royal Air Force*, finds it surprising that the lessons of the Great War, in which submarine attacks had brought Britain close to starvation and defeat in 1917, had not been learned, as preparations were made for another war with Germany. This resulted in neither the Royal Navy nor the RAF having a clear idea of how it would cope with the submarine menace. The publication concluded that, "RAF co-operation with the Navy had been overshadowed for too long by the argument over who should control the Fleet Air Arm," adding, "so little had been done that in an exercise in 1939 one 100lb anti-submarine bomb bounced off one of our own submarines with only the most minor damage".

With the advent of hostilities, while the Navy placed great reliance on ASDIC, Coastal Command found itself in the situation described by Andrew Hendrie in the first paragraph of this entry. It was a long time before matters improved to any significant degree.

The level of success against the submarines began to improve from the summer of 1942 – with the stamina and courage of the Coastal Command airmen playing a major part.

However, as late as the first months of 1943, U-boat pack attacks in the Atlantic were still meeting with considerable success. Even so, better aircraft, improved technology and the closing of the "Gap" had their effect. U-boats found it far more difficult to operate in the Atlantic in particular. As an example of successful use of new technology, on June 1 1943, a Beaufighter of No. 236 Squadron (pilot, Flying Officer M. C. Bateman), flying from Predannack, sank *U-418* with two rocket projectiles (RPs).

At this time there were frequent changes of tactics. The advantage in the U-boat battle swung between the two sides, but the momentum

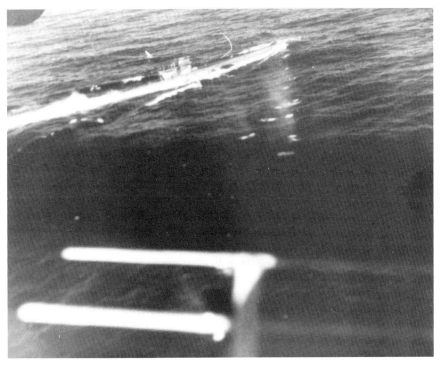

An attack on a U-boat photographed by a Coastal Command aircraft.

was now with the Allies. In the first quarter of 1944 sixty U-boats were destroyed in the Atlantic, with the loss of fifty-four friendly ships. Though this still seems a terrible total, it was a vastly better figure than the losses of 1942. German expectation of an invasion of the Continent, and therefore the need to defend it, was also a factor in reducing the number of submarines operating out to sea.

From 1940, depth charges, normally launched from Royal Navy ships, were adapted for use by Coastal Command aircraft, despite a number of disadvantages including the fact that the weapons had not been designed to be tough enough to be dropped from aircraft.

London and Stranraer flying boats could carry two depth charges externally, although the capacity of the Stranraer was reduced to one if it was fitted with a long range fuel tank. Sunderlands and Catalinas could be used to deploy four depth charges. The first occasion on which this form of attack was used against a U-boat occurred in August 1940 when a Sunderland launched one against *U-51*.

Depth charges, purpose-built for aerial use, became available. They were smaller and could be carried by types including Hudsons, Wellingtons, Whitleys and Liberators. Sunderlands and Liberators could carry eight of these devices.

"Where the German Navy was concerned, Hitler's eye was on U-boats. He had no great use for big warships and when times were bad for Germany he would suggest from time to time that they should be de-commissioned. Germany had no aircraft carriers. But he was never in doubt about the importance, and when his other strategic ideas fell into disarray he hoped that the U-boat would help to win the war for him." (Sir Maurice Dean in *The Royal Air Force and Two World Wars*).

"We also attacked U-boats though not with great success. For some reason, anti-submarine attacks had formed no part of our peacetime training. We trained entirely in reconnaissance and bombing, but with no accent on the incredibly difficult target that the diving

Briefing before an anti–submarine patrol.

U-boat was to present. It was obvious that one would have to aim a stick of bombs ahead of the last known position of the U-boat, but it was a hit and miss business, chiefly miss. In the opaque waters of the North Sea, once the conning tower had vanished from sight it was as though that big black boat had never been there." (Gron Edwards writing about No. 233 Squadron in the last months of 1939, in *Norwegian Patrol*).

Armstrong Whitworth Whitley – As a medium bomber, the Whitley first flew in March 1936. A year later operational examples of the Whitley I began to arrive at Dishforth for No. 10 Squadron in Bomber Command, where it would be a key aircraft until the advent of the "heavies". The name chosen for the new aircraft was that of the Coventry district of Whitley, the location of an Armstrong Whitworth plant.

In its early form the Whitley was fitted with two Armstrong Siddeley Tiger engines, many later examples would have power provided by Rolls Royce Merlins.

The Whitley's last operational contribution to the bomber offensive was the "thousand raid" on Cologne on May 30/31 1942, when OTU aircraft and crews were added to the attack.

Although Whitleys had been used by Coastal Command from early in the war, it was with the appearance of the Whitley GR Mk VII in late 1941 that the type made its biggest impact in the Command. The Mk VII was specifically designed as a patrol aircraft, it was fitted with ASV Mk II radar and carried additional fuel. In this form Whitleys sank a number of U-boats, before being superseded by other types.

Whitleys were also used to train glider tug pilots and paratroops, in the latter role operating from Ringway, Manchester. Further, Whitleys dropped agents and supplied resistance groups in occupied countries and – unarmed and operated by BOAC – flew supplies from Gibraltar to Malta.

"At 15.01 hours on 15th September, Whitley Q/58, flying at 6,700 ft, sighted a U-boat [*U-261*] at a distance of 7 miles. It was making 10 knots. The aircraft turned and broke cloud at 3,000 ft, then attacked from the U-boat's port quarter with five Torpex depth charges, released from 20 ft, while the U-boat was fully surfaced. The depth charges straddled it; three fell short to port, one made a direct hit on the bridge, and one fell beyond to starboard. As the explosions subsided the bows were seen sticking out of the water at an angle of about 15 degrees. The aircraft turned to make another attack. The bows of the U-boat slid under just before the release of the remaining depth charge, leaving on the surface an oil patch, about 90 yards long and 25 yards wide, in the centre of which were many bits of wood, which looked like broken up duckboard, a black object shaped like a drum and pieces of orange-coloured stuff, a foot or two across, irregular in shape and curled up at the edges like scraps of orange peel (painted plywood?). The remaining Torpex depth charge exploded in the centre of this oil and debris, 5 seconds after the bows had gone out of sight, but no further results were seen. The aircraft dropped a submarine marker, and flew

The Armstrong Whitworth Whitley in Coastal Command service.

away northward, returning to the scene twenty minutes later [see entry for "Baiting"] and then making a square search without results. The wreckage and debris seen after the main depth charge attack, together with the quantity of oil, indicate that total destruction is more than likely." (From *Coastal Command Review*, September 1942). The sinking of the U-boat was later confirmed. Torpex was an explosive introduced during the war.

Atlantic (Battle of) – This was, in part, the attempt by the German navy and air force to cut off supplies of food and other essentials to Britain, by making the passage of shipping extremely hazardous. At the same time, Britain, from the outset of the war, sought to impose a naval blockade on Germany. Though there were peaks and troughs, the Battle lasted throughout the five years and eight months of the war in Europe. It was fought in particular on the Allied side, by the navies and air forces of Britain and Canada, with convoys crossing the Atlantic from north American ports to reach Britain and Russia.

Closeness to despair came in 1942. During that year British, Allied and neutral shipping weighing almost 8,000,000 tons was sunk by enemy action.

A major role in winning the battle was taken by the cryptographers at Bletchley Park, who provided much information on the movements of U-boats. On September 6 1941, the Prime Minister went to their Buckinghamshire base to give personal thanks for what they were doing for the war effort in this and other ways. Four months earlier the ability of the Allies to wage the Battle had taken a great step forward when a party from the destroyer, HMS *Bulldog,* boarded a German submarine and captured her code books and the then current keys for the naval Enigma machines. Up to that point the enemy had believed the Enigma system unbreakable.

Coastal Command played a full part in the Battle throughout the war and steadily developed its skill and equipment during all that time.

"But how about our life-line across the Atlantic? What is to happen if so many of our merchant ships are sunk that we cannot bring in the food we need to nourish our brave people? What if the supplies of war materials and war weapons which the United States are seeking to send us in such enormous quantities should in large part be sunk on the way? What is to happen then? In February, as you may remember, that bad man in one of his raving outbursts threatened us with a terrifying increase in the numbers and activities of his U-boats and in his air-attack – not only on our Island but, thanks to his use of French and Norwegian harbours, and thanks to the denial to us of the Irish bases – upon our shipping far out into the Atlantic. We have taken and are taking all possible measures to meet this deadly attack, and we are now fighting against it with might and main. That is what is called the Battle of the Atlantic, which in order to survive we have got to win on salt water just as decisively as we had to win the Battle of Britain last August and September in the air." (Winston Churchill, on the BBC, April 27 1941).

Plotting the Battle of the Atlantic.

"We chose the BOA [Battle of the Atlantic] because it was pivotal to the success of the allied war. After the fall of Europe, the main supply route for the continued prosecution of the war was between the United States/Canada and the UK via the North Atlantic. Ultimately, it was the success of the protection of this vital sea corridor by the defeat of the German Surface and U-boat threat that enabled the massive logistic build up that led to success in North Africa, at D-Day and then through to the fall of Germany." (Royal Navy website, explaining why the service had decided to mark the seventieth anniversary of the Battle of the Atlantic in May 2013).

Atlantic Gap (Mid Ocean and Mid Atlantic Gap were amongst the other names applied to it) – The area in the middle of the Atlantic Ocean where, in the earlier part of the war, aircraft flying from Britain or North America did not have the range to protect convoys.

Gradually the "Gap" was shortened and closed by the advent of new aircraft types, the establishment of No. 30 Wing in Iceland and the setting up of US bases in Canada, Newfoundland (then independent of Canada) and Greenland.

Atlantic Star – The Atlantic Star was awarded to those involved in operations during the Battle of the Atlantic from September 3 1940 to May 8 1945. The watered ribbon of blue, white and green represents the mood of the Atlantic. The clasps, Aircrew Europe and France and Germany, can be worn with this star but not both.

Most recipients were from the Royal Navy and Merchant Navy, but RAF personnel also received the award if, having qualified for the 1939–1945 Star, they had flown operationally in the specified area for two months or had served as aircrew for four months.

The Atlantic Star.

Immediate awards were made to those who suffered death, disability or wounds as a result of service in the qualifying area and to those who received a gallantry award or mention in despatches.

Auxiliary Air Force (AAF) – Provision for an Auxiliary Air Force and Air Force Reserve was made in the Air Force (Constitution) Act of 1917. Both were part of the plans of Sir Hugh Trenchard for the development of the RAF after the Great War.

The first Auxiliary squadron to be established was No. 602 (City of Glasgow) Squadron on September 15 1925.

Many years later, Viscount Templewood, who, as Sir Samuel Hoare Bt, had peacetime and wartime spells as Air Minister, wrote, "Trenchard envisaged the Auxiliaries as a Corps d'elite, composed of the kind of young men who earlier would have been interested in horses, but who now wished to serve their country in machines. He conceived the new mechanical yeomanry with its aeroplanes based on the great centres of industry. Esprit de corps was to be the dominating force in the squadrons and each, therefore, was to have a well-equipped headquarters, mess, and distinctive life of its own. Social meetings were to be encouraged and on no account was any squadron to be regarded as a reserve for filling up regular units. The experiment was successful from the beginning. The forebodings of the doubters and critics were soon proved groundless. So far from the non-regular units damaging the reputation of the regular squadrons they actually added some of the most glorious pages to the history of the Royal Air Force during the Second World War."

Special Reserve squadrons were also set up, the first of these being No. 502 (Ulster), which began to form in May 1925.

A regular officer commanded each Special Reserve squadron, which, unlike the AAF units, had a nucleus of regulars, as well as volunteers, serving on a part time basis. By the outbreak of the Second World War, all five Special Reserve squadrons had become part of the AAF.

With the declaration of war, recruiting for the AAF ceased and all AAF personnel were transferred to the RAFVR, "for the emergency", many serving in Coastal Command.

In 1945 the decision was taken by the Air Ministry to re-form the AAF. Squadrons using former AAF number-plates generally by that time had little connection with the pre-war AAF and so were renumbered or disbanded, to enable the creation of a new auxiliary force with the original local affiliations. The re-formed AAF was established in June 1946, becoming the Royal Auxiliary Air Force (RAuxAF), by permission of King George VI, in December 1947.

The auxiliary squadrons were disbanded in 1957, but from 1979 the RAuxAF became operational again in a variety of ground roles.

Avro Anson – The Anson came into being as a civilian aircraft for use by Imperial Airways. The Avro 652, as it was then called, first flew on January 7 1935 and two examples were delivered to Imperial Airways in March the same year.

The Avro Anson.

Already A. V. Roe had received an Air Ministry requirement for a coastal reconnaissance aircraft and a modified design, the 652A, was produced. In March 1936, No. 48 Squadron, based at Manston, Kent, became the first RAF unit to operate what was now the Anson. Eventually twenty further Coastal Command squadrons received Ansons.

In RAF service the Anson I had two Armstrong-Siddeley Cheetah IX radial piston engines, with a maximum speed of 188 mph and a service ceiling of 19,000 ft. The range was 790 miles. Armament consisted of one 0.303 in forward firing machine gun and another in a dorsal turret; up to 360lb of bombs could be carried.

The Anson was taken out of front line service in 1942, but continued, not least as a trainer and communications aircraft, to serve the RAF until 1968. Production had ended in 1952.

Avro Lancaster – Though the Lancaster is rightly associated in particular with Bomber Command, it was briefly a Coastal Command aircraft too during the war and served in peacetime. It would have added considerably to the ability of the Command to perform a number of its tasks, had it been made available in larger numbers and on a permanent basis. Here was an example of "Cinderella Service" treatment.

In 1940 the Avro Chief Designer Roy Chadwick and his team were working on a four-engine version of the Avro Manchester, two-engine bomber, which would be equipped with Rolls Royce Merlin engines. With the Merlin badly needed for Hurricane and Spitfire fighters, the Air Ministry did not encourage the project at first. Eventually, a request to go ahead with the design was made, with the stipulation that as many Manchester components as possible should be used.

The first flight of a prototype Lancaster took place on January 9 1941. On December 24 1941 No. 44 Squadron, based at Waddington, Lincolnshire, became the first squadron in Bomber Command to receive Lancasters. The earliest Lancaster participation in an operation occurred on March 3 1942 when four of the type from No. 44 Squadron laid mines in the Heligoland Bight between the mouth of the River Elbe and the Heligoland Islands.

Over 7,000 Lancasters were built and fifty-seven Bomber Command squadrons were equipped with them during the Second World War.

Today the Lancaster lives on most prominently in the shape of PA474, the aircraft operated by the Battle of Britain Memorial Flight from Coningsby, in varying guises.

Nearby, at the former Bomber Command airfield at East Kirkby, the Lincolnshire Aviation Heritage Centre offers the chance to taxi in Lancaster NX611, "Just Jane". There are hopes that this aircraft will fly again.

During the Second World War, Coastal Command made representations to be allocated Lancasters, but it was not until after hostilities had ended that Lancasters were formally added to the Command. During the war itself some Lancasters were loaned to Coastal Command, but the pressure to keep all of these outstanding aircraft focused on the bomber offensive was always very strong. The Lancaster represents one of the key instances where Coastal Command did not reach the top of the list of Air Ministry priorities.

Azores – A remote group of volcanic islands in the north Atlantic, owned by Portugal, which is often referred to as Britain's oldest ally. After diplomatic pressure, the Portuguese agreed to a British base being established in the Azores from October 1943. Thus Coastal Command aircraft were able to operate in what had previously been known as the "Azores Gap".

To generations of British school children the Azores were perhaps more associated with sixteenth century maritime conflict – the heroic, yet controversial, "last stand" in 1591 of the *Revenge* (Drake's ship when he sailed against the Armada), as immortalised by Alfred Tennyson in the poem beginning:-

"At Flores in the Azores Sir Richard Grenville lay,
And a pinnace, like a fluttered bird, came flying from far away:
'Spanish ships of war at sea! We have sighted fifty-three!'
Then sware Lord Thomas Howard: 'Fore God I am no coward;
But I cannot meet them here, for my ships are out of gear,
And half my men are sick. I must fly, but follow quick.
We are six ships of the line; can we fight with fifty-three?'

"Then spake Sir Richard Grenville: 'I know you are no coward;
You fly them for a moment to fight with them again.
But I've ninety men and more that are lying sick ashore.
I should count myself the coward if I left them, my Lord Howard,
To these Inquisition dogs and the devildoms of Spain.'"

B

Baiting – A tactic first used in the Great War and adopted again a quarter of a century later, in which an aircraft would leave the scene of an apparently inconclusive attack, where the U-boat had dived. The aircraft would return later, making as much use as possible of cloud or sun to obscure its approach in the hope of catching its target on the surface and vulnerable to a further assault.

Bandstand – Name given by Allied airmen to platforms added beside the conning towers of U-boats to carry extra defensive armament. The Germans referred to them as "der wintergarten" (the winter garden).

Battle of Britain – The term "Battle of Britain" originated from the speech made by the Prime Minister, Winston Churchill, in the House of Commons on June 18 1940.

In the key passage he said, "What General Weygand called the Battle of France is over. I expect that the Battle of Britain is about to begin. Upon this battle depends the survival of Christian civilization. Upon it depends our own British life, and the long continuity of our institutions and our Empire. The whole fury and might of the enemy must very soon be turned on us. Hitler knows that he will have to break us in this Island or lose the war. If we can stand up to him, all Europe may be free and the life of the world may move forward into broad, sunlit uplands. But if we fail, then the whole world, including the United States, including all that we have known and cared for, will sink into the abyss of a new Dark Age made more sinister, and perhaps more protracted, by the lights of perverted science. Let us therefore brace ourselves to our duties, and so bear ourselves that, if the British Empire and its Commonwealth last for a thousand years, men will still say, this was their finest hour."

On August 20 1940, in a further speech in the House of Commons, Churchill declared:

"The gratitude of every home in our Island, in our Empire, and indeed throughout the world, except in the abodes of the guilty, goes out to the British airmen who, undaunted by odds, unwearied in their constant challenge and mortal danger, are turning the tide of the World War by their prowess and by their devotion. Never in the field of human conflict was so much owed by so many to so few. All hearts go out to the fighter pilots, whose brilliant actions we see with our own eyes day after day; but we must never forget that all the time, night after night, month after month, our bomber squadrons travel far into Germany, find their targets in the darkness by the highest navigational skill, aim their attacks, often under the heaviest fire, often with serious loss, with deliberate careful discrimination, and inflict shattering blows upon the whole of the technical and war-making structure of the Nazi power. On no part of the Royal Air Force does the weight of the war fall more heavily than on the daylight bombers, who will play an invaluable part in the case of invasion and whose unflinching zeal it has been necessary in the meanwhile on numerous occasions to restrain."

The precise meaning of these words has been debated ever since, though Churchill wrote in his *The Second World War* that in referring to "so few", he had meant the fighter pilots. Nonetheless, this speech can be taken as a tribute to Coastal Command, as well as Fighter and Bomber Commands. Certainly Coastal Command, in the Battle of the Barges and in other ways, played its part in winning the Battle of Britain.

During the Battle (officially lasting from July 19 to October 31 1940) three of Coastal Command's Blenheim squadrons, Nos. 235, 236 and 248, served under Fighter Command control and their aircrew who made one authorised operational sortie, while in the Fighter fold and between the official dates, eventually qualified for the "immediate" award of the 1939–1945 Star with Battle of Britain Clasp. This Clasp was the only one awarded with the Star for many years, until the inauguration of the Clasp for Bomber Command aircrew. Operational service with Fighter Command by two other Coastal Command squadrons, Nos. 53 and 59, was originally intended to be a qualification for the Battle of Britain Clasp, but these squadrons were subsequently deleted from the list, apparently, at least in part, because they operated the bomber version of the Blenheim.

"Because we lacked the speeds of the single-engine fighter aircraft, our duties were, basically, aerodrome protection, either at Bircham Newton, or as one of six aircraft on detachment at Thorney Island (near Portsmouth) or St Eval (near Newquay). This involvement meant that whenever an enemy raid was about to commence we became airborne and circled the particular aerodrome at which we were stationed, at 4,000–6,000 feet.

"Another one of our duties was to act as fighter protection on sorties made across the Channel by both bomber and torpedo aircraft. One of the most hair raising of these occurred on 11 September 1940 when six aircraft led by Flight Lieutenant F. W. Flood (a twenty-five-year-old who had transferred to the RAF from the Royal Australian Air Force in 1936) took off from Bircham Newton at about 14.30 hours, to rendezvous over Detling, Kent with six Albacores of the Fleet Air Arm to escort them to Calais to attack some of the many ships packed in and around the port.

"The Albacores, each carrying a torpedo (which reduced their speed to a little over 100 mph) went in low ('wave hopping') and we flew in a 'box' around them at about 2,000–2,500 feet. Up to this time it had been a glorious summer afternoon, but we were now greeted with dozens of puffs of black smoke, anti-aircraft shells exploding all around us and then we were attacked by twenty-five plus Messerschmitt 109s (the official entry in Air Chief Marshal Dowding's diary kept at Bentley Priory, HQ of Fighter Command, shows this).

A photograph of Owen V. Burns circa 1940.

"Fortunately for us their attack lasted only a few minutes – an explanation could be that they were returning from an attack in the south of England. We managed to get back minus three Albacores and two Blenheims, one of which was that flown by Flight Lieutenant Flood." (Flight Lieutenant Owen Burns, in 1940 a Sergeant Wireless Operator/Air Gunner with No. 235 Squadron, quoted in the supplement, *The Last of The Few,* to *Britain at War*, April 2012).

"On August 11 [Sergeant William] Wilson was a member of the crew of a Blenheim, one of three from 235, returning after escorting a reconnaissance Blenheim to the French coast. On the return flight they were attacked by two Bf 109s. One fighter was shot down and the other driven off by concentrated fire from the Blenheim gunners.

"In another action on August 18, Wilson was involved in shooting down a Ju 87. For these two actions, he was awarded the DFM (22/10/40)." (From *Men of the Battle of Britain* by Kenneth G. Wynn).

John Terraine in *Right of the Line* argued that it is a "serious blemish in existing accounts [of the Battle of Britain] that British air losses in the fight for national survival almost never include those of Bomber and Coastal Commands." Terraine went on to acknowledge the difficulty of separating sorties directly related to "survival" from other operations, but offered his own approximate calculation. This amounted to 118 aircraft of Bomber Command and 130 of Coastal Command lost in contributing directly to the outcome of the Battle of Britain.

One place where the contribution continues to be recognised is on the Roll of Honour presented to Westminster Abbey by Sir Bruce Ingram in 1947. As well as Fighter Command aircrew lost in the Battle, the parchment contains the names of other aircrew lost at that time, including those of Coastal Command.

Battle of the Barges – As the Battle of Britain was fought by RAF Fighter Command (between July 10 and October 31 1940), so Bomber Command, Coastal Command and the Fleet Air Arm were engaged in

Many invasions barges caught in Boulogne harbour.

"The Battle of the Barges", which came to its height in September. Both struggles were means of preventing a German invasion of southern England. For Fighter Command the objective was to deny the Luftwaffe air superiority over the Channel and the potential invasion area.

Coastal Command was part of the effort to destroy the fleet of barges and other craft and facilities that the Germans would use to bring their forces to the English coast. Much heroism was shown and many successful attacks made. There was, of course, no invasion.

Beaverbrook, Lord (1879–1964) – William Maxwell Aitken was born in Canada. In Britain he became a newspaper magnate and a Unionist MP. He was knighted in 1911 and served in the cabinet as Chancellor of the Duchy of Lancaster. He was awarded a peerage and took his title from a small Canadian community, close to his childhood home.

A portrait of Lord Beaverbrook dated 1943.

On May 14 1940 Churchill appointed Beaverbrook Minister of Aircraft Production and he joined the War Cabinet in August. He achieved much, though he was often at loggerheads with colleagues and the RAF, a favourite expression being "Bloody Air Marshals". He resigned the post in April 1941, but took further high Government appointments.

Beaverbrook's elder son, Squadron Leader the Hon. Max Aitken, was CO of No. 601 Squadron, equipped with Hurricanes, at the start of the Battle of Britain. Later in the war he commanded the Banff Mosquito Strike Wing and left the RAF as a Group Captain. On the death of his father he disclaimed the peerage, but took the Baronetcy which Beaverbrook had also received, thereby becoming known as Sir Max Aitken Bt. He died in 1985.

The third Lord Beaverbrook (son of Sir Max) was in 2009 appointed Honorary Inspector General Royal Auxiliary Air Force, in the rank of Air Vice-Marshal.

Bircham Newton – In the First World War the airfield at Bircham Newton, Norfolk was used, from 1916, to train pilots to fly fighters and then as a base for bombers. The bomber role continued until 1936 when Coastal Command took over and Bircham Newton became a significant contributor to the wartime operations of No. 16 Group. Fairey Swordfish of the Fleet Air Arm also flew from the airfield. Satellites were established at Langham and Docking.

Langham was regarded as an independent station from 1942, and from 1944 was home to the "Anzac" Wing, Nos. 455 (Australian) Squadron and 489 (New Zealand) Squadron operating "Torbeaus". The Wing was replaced by meteorological squadrons. Langham closed in the 1960s.

Docking was considered particularly suitable for night operations and also housed "met" units. With the coming of peace flying ended at the airfield.

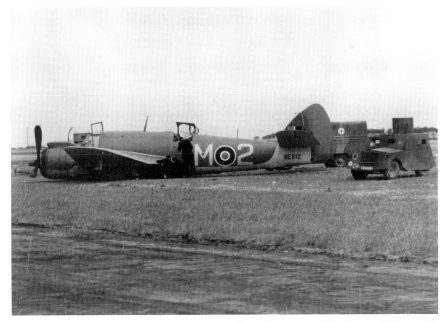

On May 14 1944, this Beaufighter of No. 455 Squadron, part of the Anzac Wing, made an emergency landing at Langham. It had been hit by flak whilst returning from an op to Borkum. Flying Officer Masson and Flight Sergeant Knight escaped.

After the war Bircham Newton left Coastal Command and was put to various uses. Closure occurred in 1962. However, in 1965, the Tripartite Evaluation Squadron of the Central Fighter Establishment, West Raynham used the former airfield as a landing ground for the Hawker Siddeley Kestrel vertical/short take-off and landing aircraft.

There is now the RAF Bircham Newton Heritage Centre, in premises provided by the Construction Industry Training Board, which holds regular open days.

"There were far too many visiting units flying from Bircham Newton during WW2 to mention them all by name. However, some early visitors will be mentioned because of the heroics they performed and the losses they sustained in the early years of the forgotten anti-shipping campaign conducted against enemy convoys, ports and airfields across the North Sea, particularly along the Dutch coast and Friesian Islands. This campaign was conducted by 235 Squadron (flying Blenheims), 500 Squadron (flying Ansons and Hudsons), 320 (Dutch) Squadron (flying Hudsons), 407 (Canadian) Squadron (flying Hudsons) and other squadrons." (From the website of the RAF Bircham Newton Memorial Project).

Biscay (Bay of) – The name given in English to the gulf in the Atlantic Ocean, running along the west coast of France from Brest and along the north coast of Spain to Cape Ortegal. It has a reputation for providing particularly testing weather conditions. The word "Biscay" comes from a province in the Spanish Basque region. Coastal Command saw much action over the Bay against German shipping and U-boats. The "Battle of the Bay" was sometimes referred to as an attempt to prevent U-boats sailing from French ports to reach the Atlantic hunting grounds.

Bismarck – German battleship launched in February 1939 and named in honour of Otto von Bismarck (Otto Eduard Leopold, Prince of Bismarck, Duke of Lauenburg, 1815–1898), the first President of a unified Germany and a dominant figure in European statesmanship for many years.

In May 1941 the *Bismarck*, accompanied by the battle cruiser, *Prinz Eugen*, ventured out of port on Operation *Rheinübung* (Rhine Exercise), tasked to attack British shipping in the Atlantic, thus reducing the level of supplies reaching Britain from North America.

British warships attempted to block their passage and the Battle of the Denmark Strait was fought, during which the Royal Navy battle cruiser, HMS *Hood*, was sunk with only three survivors. The *Bismarck* was damaged as was the Royal Navy battleship, HMS *Prince of Wales*.

As well as being a great tragedy and loss of a major ship, the sinking of HMS *Hood* was a considerable propaganda and morale setback for

Britain. A large air and sea search was mounted to find *Bismarck* and then destroy her.

On May 26 the ship was sighted, heading for Brest, by a Catalina of No. 209 Squadron. The Royal Navy's Force H was in the best position to intervene. Fleet Air Arm Fairey Swordfish from HMS *Ark Royal* were despatched to attack the *Bismarck*, though some launched their torpedoes by mistake at the heavy cruiser HMS *Sheffield*, without inflicting damage. After the *Sheffield* engaged the *Bismarck*, two torpedoes from Swordfish struck the German ship, one of which rendered her un-manoeuvrable.

Various other ships attacked the *Bismarck* and scuttling was set in motion on board. Eventually torpedoes fired by HMS *Dorsetshire* finished off the German battleship. Some survivors were rescued.

The Catalina from No. 209 Squadron, skippered by Flying Officer Dennis Briggs, that sighted the *Bismarck*, in the Atlantic. The co-pilot was Ensign Leonard B. Smith, United States Navy, one of a number of Americans flying with Coastal Command at the time.

The atmosphere of determination to achieve victory over the *Bismarck* was portrayed in the film *Sink the Bismarck* (1960), although the major characters played by stars such as Kenneth More and Dana Wynter were largely fictitious. The Captain of the *Prince of Wales* was played by Esmond Knight who had been virtually blinded serving on the ship in real life during the Battle of the Denmark Strait.

"Meanwhile the Sunderland from Iceland had arrived in the neighbourhood of the *Suffolk* and, on sighting this ship, saw at the same time the flash of gunfire well ahead. 'As we closed,' says the captain in his report, 'two columns, each of two ships in line ahead, were seen to be steering on parallel courses at an estimated range of 12 miles between the columns. Heavy gunfire was being exchanged and the leading ship of the port column was on fire in two places, one fire being at the base of the bridge superstructure and the other farther

Flying Officer Dennis Briggs.

aft. In spite of these large conflagrations she appeared to be firing at least one turret forward and one aft.'

"At first the captain of the Sunderland could not identify the burning ship. He turned towards the starboard column and noticed that the second of two ships comprising it was making a considerable amount of smoke and that oil escaping from her was leaving a broad track upon the surface of the sea. He approached nearer and as he did so the ship on fire in the column to port blew up." (Coastal Command witnesses the end of HMS *Hood*, as recorded in the official Air Ministry account of the Command's war to that point, published in 1942).

Blackburn Botha – The twin-engine Botha entered operational service with the RAF in 1940, having been designed for torpedo bombing and reconnaissance roles. However, it was found to have serious defects, one of which, remarkably given its purposes, was poor visibility to the side or rear. Only No. 608 (North Riding) Squadron used Bothas operationally, briefly and mainly on convoy patrols. The "Bloody Botha" was a not infrequent appellation.

Once removed from front line service the Botha was used for training and as a target tug.

Blockade Runners – Term often applied during the Second World War to ships seeking to evade the Royal Navy's blockade of German ports. The difficulty of maintaining this blockade increased once French ports such as Bordeaux became available to the Germans. As air superiority was gained by Coastal Command over the Bay of Biscay, so the difficulty for the Germans greatly increased.

Boeing B-17 Flying Fortress – The B-17 was created following a US Army specification of 1934 when the requirement was for a long-range, high-altitude, daylight bomber. Though it went on to become one of the most famous bombers of all time, the B-17's mainstream

A Boeing B-17 Flying Fortress of No. 220 Squadron on patrol from RAF Benbecula in the Outer Hebrides in 1943.

career in RAF Bomber Command, with No. 90 Squadron, was brief, there were a number of problems and the design was already looking dated compared with other four-engine bombers which were entering service.

With Bomber Command not finding a further use for the aircraft, it became available to Coastal Command in significant numbers and served with a range of squadrons. The remaining aircraft in Bomber Command went to No. 220 Squadron and were used on anti-submarine patrols over the Atlantic – the Fortress had a range of 2,000 miles. Other uses were long-range reconnaissance, air sea rescue and meteorological flights.

Meanwhile, the Fortress continued to fly daylight bombing missions over Europe with the USAAF. The crews suffered terrible casualties. Their torment produced arguably one of the great novels describing aerial combat in the Second World War – *The War Lover* by John Hersey.

An example of a successful Flying Fortress pilot in Coastal Command was Leslie Clark of No. 206 Squadron. On March 19 1943 he was the captain of a Fortress, operating from Benbecula in the Outer Hebrides. A U-boat was detected close to a convoy sailing from Halifax, Nova Scotia, to Britain. Clark's aircraft straddled *U-384* with four depth charges, causing the submarine to sink. In the first half of 1943 Clark was credited with damaging two other U-boats.

His service also included taking part in Bomber Command's third "thousand bomber" raid, with Bremen as the target. His Hudson bombed successfully.

Leslie Clark was awarded the DFC and was a Squadron Leader when he left the RAF in 1946. He died in 2012.

Bomber Command (Coastal Command relationship with) – The roles and fortunes of Coastal and Bomber Commands touched each other on frequent occasions during the war.

In the very early days of hostilities, for instance, Coastal's strength was increased by loans of squadrons from Bomber Command and elsewhere.

In 1940 there was concern (as there had been before the war) from some senior Bomber Command officers (of whom Air Vice-Marshal Arthur Harris, leading No. 5 Group was one) that air sea rescue arrangements were inadequate. This led to Bomber Command developing its own rescue capability, starting with the provision of a new dinghy, to be dropped from Hampdens to men in the sea. Later, as Deputy Chief of the Air Staff, Harris would be a force in establishing the full air sea rescue service within Coastal Command.

From early 1942 Harris was Air Officer, Commanding in Chief, Bomber Command and often espoused the view that too many aircraft and men were being diverted to Coastal Command (and the Middle East).

Determined to show that Bomber Command could be welded into a war-winning weapon and needing to achieve positive results quickly, Harris devised the concept of "Thousand Bomber" attacks on German cities. He secured the support of Air Chief Marshal Portal, Chief of the Air Staff, as well as the Prime Minister. Initially support was also given by Admiral Sir Dudley Pound, the First Sea Lord, and Air Marshal Joubert at Coastal Command agreed to provide 250 aircraft. However, the demands of fighting the Battle of the Atlantic were too great to risk heavy losses and the Admiralty ensured that the offer was withdrawn.

On the night of May 30/31 1942, Cologne was attacked and the figure of 1,000 was passed by using aircraft from Fighter and Army Co-operation Commands and by drawing on the training units of Bomber Command, using experienced instructors and those under training. The raid was considered a success.

There were further "thousand" raids on Essen and Bremen. In the latter, 100 aircraft from Coastal Command participated.

"In all, 19 new squadrons were formed in the Command during 1942, and 13 of these were taken from us. And of the new squadrons that were left to us, three were on more or less permanent loan to Coastal Command and engaged in anti-submarine patrols. From May 1942, to the end of February 1943, additional aircraft lent to Coastal Command made 1,000 sorties while engaged in this work." (Marshal of the RAF Sir Arthur Harris in *Bomber Offensive*).

In early 1943, after intense protest by Harris, Bomber Command delayed its main offensive against the Ruhr, to spend two months attacking U-boat pens on the French Atlantic coast. Harris predicted that their concrete construction would prove impenetrable and the results of the campaign largely confirmed his view.

A particularly celebrated contribution by Bomber Command to the war against the U-boats had come in April 1942 when 12 Lancasters from Nos. 44 and 97 Squadrons flew in daylight to attack the M.A.N.

factory at Augsburg, Bavaria, where engines for submarines were manufactured. The factory was hit but the cost was high, with seven of the aircraft failing to return. The leader of the raid, Squadron Leader John Nettleton of No. 44 Squadron, survived and was awarded the Victoria Cross.

Bowhill, Air Chief Marshal Sir Frederick William (1880–1960) – Bowhill was born in India and was the son of an Army officer. The future of AOC in C of Coastal Command spent 16 years in the Merchant Navy. He was on leave from the P & O company and a Lieutenant in the Royal Naval Reserve when he learned to fly in 1912.

In the following year he joined the then Naval Wing of the Royal Flying Corps as a Lieutenant RN. He was given command of the requisitioned ship HMS *Empress*, operating as a sea plane carrier

Air Chief Marshal Sir Frederick Bowhill.

and with her took part in the Cuxhaven raid of December 25 1914. Bowhill later commanded the RNAS contingent in Mesopotamia. He went to East Africa and, in 1918, was appointed DSO for his services there.

The citation for the award stated that it was, "in recognition of his valuable services as Commanding Officer of the RNAS employed in connection with military operations in East Africa. It is due to his experience and unceasing labour that his small unit of RNAS has been of such assistance to the military operations. He has instilled a high sense of discipline into those under his orders."

Bowhill joined the newly-formed RAF as a Lieutenant Colonel (the RAF ranks familiar today were not introduced until 1919), commanded a Wing in the Mediterranean and received a bar to the DSO. By the end of 1919, Bowhill was a Wing Commander, with a permanent RAF commission.

He served in Somaliland in actions against the "Mad Mullah" and, back in the UK, held a senior staff appointment at Coastal Area. He went to the Middle East, had a stint at the Air Ministry, then, in 1931, as an Air Vice-Marshal, he became Air Officer Commanding, Fighting Area, Air Defence of Great Britain. Two years later he joined the Air Council, as Air Member for Personnel. Bowhill's next appointment, in 1937, was as Air Officer Commanding in Chief, Coastal Command, a role he performed until 1941.

"Ginger" Bowhill (also made highly recognisable by his formidable eyebrows) then took charge of the nascent Ferry Command. Based in Canada, he exerted considerable charm, as did his wife who was present as a WAAF officer, to maintain good relations with the civilians who had previously run the Ferry operation. From 1943 he commanded Transport Command, into which Ferry Command was incorporated. Retirement came in 1945.

Later appointments included being Chief Aeronautical Adviser to the Ministry of Civil Aviation and as a Younger Brother of Trinity House.

"Its [Coastal Command] equipment had improved out of all recognition. The nineteen squadrons of 1939 had grown to 40. The average range of its aircraft had doubled. Efficient torpedo bombers and long range fighters – though still all too few – had taken their place in the line of battle. More than half the aircraft of the Command had been fitted with … an improved ASV … Experiment with camouflage of Coastal aircraft and the development of an airborne searchlight were about to be crowned with success. It was with the knowledge that many, though by no means all, of the basic problems and difficulties had been overcome that Bowhill handed over to his successor, Air Marshal Sir Philip Joubert." (Denis Richards writing in *The Royal Air Force 1939–1945*).

Bristol Beaufighter – An aircraft which, despite its success, was developed in haste to meet a need for a well-armed night and long-range escort fighter. It carried a crew of two and was based on the

Bristol Beaufighters of the North Coates Strike Wing attacked and sank this German Navy magnetic mine detonating vessel on April 20 1944. This mast-level photograph was captured shortly before an explosion devastated *Sperrbrecher 102* off the Dutch coast.

Bristol company's Beaufort and Blenheim types. The aircraft became popularly known as the "Beau".

In the latter stages of the Battle of Britain the Beaufighter began to appear on Nos. 25 and 29 Squadrons in Fighter Command. During the night Blitz of 1940/1941 the Beaufighter, using Airborne Interception radar, proved a significant threat to German bombers.

Modified for Coastal Command, as a long range fighter, the Mk I C Beaufighter often carried bombs. As the war moved on the Beaufighter became particularly associated with Coastal Command.

Beaufighters were also used by the Royal Australian Air Force on anti-shipping strikes. Beaufighters Xs were built in Australia and, known as TF Mk 21a, served with the RAAF, playing an important role in the advance of the Allies in the East Indies. Beaufighters appearing at low level not only did the Japanese material damage, but affected morale. To the Japanese they became known as "Whispering Death".

The torpedo-carrying Mk VI C variant, delivered to Coastal Command from 1942, carried torpedoes and was referred to as the "Torbeau".

Bristol Beaufort – Designed to meet a requirement for a land-based torpedo and reconnaissance aircraft, the Beaufort was a descendant of the Blenheim. Like the Blenheim, the name given to the type had stately connections, being a tribute to the Duke of Beaufort whose seat was Badminton House, not far from the Bristol company's works. Unusually for an English Duke, the title relates to a French location – Beaufort Castle in Champagne.

The Beaufort aircraft was ordered straight from the drawing board. A crew of four was carried. The first flight was in October 1938. However, there were delays, particularly with overheating of the Bristol Taurus engines. It was not until the beginning of 1940 that Beauforts started to enter operational service with No. 22 Squadron in Coastal Command.

Armourers load a Mark XII aerial torpedo into a Bristol Beaufort of No. 42 Squadron at RAF Leuchars, 1941.

In service Beauforts were more often used for delivering bombs than torpedoes. They were also utilised for minelaying. German capital ships were targeted on a number of occasions – see entries for "Channel Dash" and "Victoria Cross".

The Beaufort left front line service in Coastal Command in 1942, but continued to serve in overseas theatres.

An asset of the Beaufort was its strength and, at the time of its introduction, there were claims that it was the fastest medium bomber in the world. However, there were frequent accidents, probably due in part to the hasty training provided for early Beaufort crews, given the anxiety to get the aircraft into service as quickly as possible.

Bristol Blenheim – An aircraft which eventually served with the RAF as both a fighter and a bomber. The Blenheim (named in honour of the home of the Dukes of Marlborough, which was also the birthplace of Winston Churchill) was developed from a private project initiated by Lord Rothermere to produce an aircraft for his own use.

When Rothermere started to pursue the idea it turned out that Frank Barnwell of the Bristol Aeroplane Company already had on paper the outline of such an aircraft. The Bristol Type 142 first flew in the spring of 1935. Its speed was a major reason why it generated much attention. The Air Ministry placed an order for a military version, featuring a bomb bay, bomb aimer's position and dorsal gun turret. Blenheim 1s began to join RAF squadrons in 1937, with further publicity accruing when No. 114 Squadron appeared in its new aircraft at that year's Hendon air display.

The Blenheim IV was developed in part to meet a requirement for an improved aircraft for coastal reconnaissance.

An early appearance of the Blenheim in Coastal Command involved "Trade Protection" squadrons, four of which were established as part of

Bristol Blenheims of Coastal Command's No. 254 Squadron in formation.

Fighter Command. These were Nos. 235, 236, 248 and 254 Squadrons and, in 1940, they moved between Fighter and Coastal Commands.

Other squadrons to operate Blenheims in Coastal Command included Nos. 53, 59, 86, 143, 233, 252, 272, 404, 407, 489 and 521.

Duties included escorting friendly ships and civilian aircraft, attacking those being used by the enemy, as well as enemy aircraft and watching over Allied airmen in the sea awaiting rescue.

In 1942 the Blenheim was being replaced in Coastal Command service by newer types.

Blenheims served widely with overseas air forces, one result of this was that some Blenheims flew in opposition to the Allies with the Romanian Air Force.

A "friendly fire" incident involving Blenheims being mistaken for German bombers occurred to No. 235 Squadron (then under Fighter Command control) on August 24 1940. After a major raid on Portsmouth, three Blenheims were attacked over the airfield at Thorney Island, Sussex, by Hurricanes of No. 1 (RCAF) Squadron. One of the No. 235 Squadron machines fell into Bracklesham Bay. The skipper, Pilot Officer David Woodger, was never found and is commemorated at Runnymede. The body of his eighteen-year-old Wireless Operator/ Air Gunner, Sergeant Danny Wright, was recovered. He now lies in Chasetown (St Ann) churchyard, Staffordshire, with, on his CWGC headstone, the words, "Thy will be done".

C

Channel Dash – "A national humiliation which shocked the British people and every part of the services concerned." (John Terraine in *The Right of the Line*).

In early February 1942 the German battleships *Scharnhorst* and *Gneisenau* were at the French port of Brest in Brittany. Also there was the heavy cruiser *Prinz Eugen*. They were subjected to air attacks and Hitler ordered that they return to Germany. A decision was taken that they would risk passing through the Strait of Dover, rather than making the longer trip via the Denmark Strait.

On February 11 the three ships, with a very large escort of destroyers and other craft, set off. The Luftwaffe mounted a major operation to provide aerial cover. The British naval and air force response throughout Operation *Cerebus*, as the Germans named it, was ineffective and the force reached Germany two days later. One reason for the British failure was that planning for what was known to them as Operation *Fuller* was based on the assumption that any passage of the Strait of Dover by the enemy ships would be at night. In fact, the fleet passed through the Strait in daylight on February 12.

Operation *Fuller* involved the use of Royal Navy ships, the Fleet Air Arm, and Bomber, Coastal and Fighter Commands, as well as shore batteries. Coastal Command was expected to mount torpedo attacks, under protection from fighters. Hudsons would seek to draw anti-aircraft fire away from the torpedo bombers.

The British had expected the breakout for months yet still found themselves caught by surprise as various possible warnings of what was happening failed to materialise.

Hudsons of No. 407 Squadron dropped 250lb bombs, suffering casualties in the process, but their attack was, unsurprisingly, ineffective. Beauforts of No. 217 Squadron fired torpedoes with no reported effect.

Coastal batteries opened fire and destroyers and motor torpedo boats went into action. The destroyer, HMS *Worcester* was badly damaged and suffered many casualties, but managed to return to Harwich.

However, the attack that is remembered by history is the one mounted by six Fairey Swordfish torpedo bombers of No. 825 Naval Air Squadron, led by Lieutenant Commander Eugene Esmonde. Forced to attack in daylight and with less fighter protection than had been promised, all six Swordfish were shot down.

The day before the attack Esmonde had been at Buckingham Palace to receive the DSO from the King. The decoration had been awarded for his leadership of a Swordfish attack on the *Bismarck*, following the Battle of the Denmark Strait. Esmonde was not one of the five Swordfish airmen rescued from the Channel after the *Fuller* sortie and he received a posthumous VC. The initial recommendation came from an RAF officer, Wing Commander Tom Gleave, Officer Commanding, RAF Manston, from where Esmonde and his men had taken off. Gleave would later say that his recommendation was accepted with such alacrity that he deeply regretted not putting forward more names for the VC. The four surviving officers received the DSO, the one rating the CGM and those who were killed were Mentioned in Despatches.

Today a memorial to all personnel who took part in Operation *Fuller* stands in the Memorial Gardens, Marine Parade, Dover and memorials dedicated to No. 825 Naval Air Squadron are to be found at Pier Yard, Ramsgate Royal Harbour and at the Spitfire and Hurricane Memorial Museum, Manston.

Cinderella Service – As men of the Fourteenth Army in Burma liked to refer to themselves as the "Forgotten Army", so veterans of Coastal Command are wont to think of themselves as having been part of the "Cinderella Service". It should be remembered that in most versions of the folk story of Cinderella, the unconsidered and put-down girl, does eventually achieve a triumph through attending the ball. Though the men of Coastal Command often saw themselves as at the end of the queue for aircraft and equipment, as well as credit for achievement, they nonetheless lived on in the knowledge that they had made a major contribution to winning the war.

The origin of the term may be in a remark by A. V. Alexander, First Lord of the Admiralty, during a meeting of the War Cabinet Defence Committee in November 1940. Alexander was recorded as referring to Coastal Command as "The Cinderella of the RAF".

The epithet quickly gained currency. In more recent years the word "Cinderella" was deployed in relation to Coastal Command a number of times in John Terraine's deservedly much quoted book, *The Right of the Line* and the Coastal Command historian, Andrew Hendrie used *The Cinderella Service* as the title of a book.

Albert Victor (A. V.) Alexander (1885–1965) became Earl Alexander of Hillsborough after the war. He was born in Somerset, the son of a blacksmith and came to prominence as a co-operator and a Labour politician. In the First World War he served in the Artists' Rifles and was a posting officer. Despite no relevant background, he spent much of his political career concerned with naval affairs and was three times First Lord of the Admiralty. He developed such expertise that apparently Mussolini, on meeting Alexander, assumed that he was a former naval officer.

In May 1940 Alexander succeeded Churchill at the Admiralty after Churchill became Prime Minister. "A V" continued in his post for the rest of the war. Alexander's biography was written by the former Labour MP John Tilley under the title, *Churchill's Favourite Socialist*.

"In my work at Coastal Command I was called upon to exercise a more single-minded concentration than I had known previously in any of my work. The operations were fought as intensely as any others carried out by the Royal Air Force, but security made no allowance for public information. I do not say that was wrong, but it did mean that we worked more alone, standing on guard, and doing it quietly and without any fanfares." (Marshal of the Royal Air Force Lord Douglas of Kirtleside, AO C in C, Coastal Command, 1944–1945, writing in *Years of Command*, 1966).

"The Fleet Air Arm, handed over to the Royal Navy in 1937, was small and its equipment inferior. The shore-based squadrons of Coastal Command were poorly equipped and their armament and tactics were elementary. The importance of the torpedo had been under estimated." (Sir Maurice Dean writing of the situation in 1939 in *The Air Force in Two World Wars*).

At that juncture, as a civil servant, Dean was in the air staff secretariat. His long career in the Air Ministry included, in 1930, handling the telephone call from one of the few survivors of the crash of the *R101* airship, who was reporting what had happened.

Circus – Term for bombers, with heavy fighter escort, sent over occupied Europe with the intention of bringing the Luftwaffe to combat. Often the bombing aircraft were provided by Coastal Command. In the period following the changes amongst RAF Commanders in late 1940, this type of operation was seen as a means of implementing the offensive role for the RAF which Lord Trenchard continued to advocate, long after he had ceased to be Chief of the Air Staff.

Coastal Command – At the time of the RAF expansion plan of 1935, five Home Commands were created to replace Air Defence of Great Britain which had been established in 1925. These were Coastal, Bomber, Training, Maintenance and Fighter Commands. The changes came at a time when what was known as "Scheme C" was being implemented, at the centre of which was the build up by 1942 to a force of seventy bomber and thirty-five fighter squadrons based in the UK.

In December 1937, Air Marshal Sir Frederick Bowhill, as Air Officer Commanding in Chief, was told that the primary role of Coastal Command would be, "trade protection, reconnaissance and co-operation with the Royal Navy".

The Royal Navy was "confident that with its ASDIC [an underwater detecting device using sound waves, named after the Allied Submarine Detection Investigation Committee] capability it could deal with the submarine threat and therefore would only require limited air support in the anti-submarine role. However, the Navy did feel threatened by the possibility of German commerce raiders (pocket battle ships and battle cruisers) breaking out from the Baltic ports, via the North Sea, into the Atlantic to harass the sea lanes." (*A Brief History of the Royal Air Force*, HMSO).

At the outbreak of war in 1939 Coastal Command consisted of three groups, No. 15, with headquarters at Plymouth, No. 16 (Chatham) and No. 18 (Rosyth). These groups included thirteen squadrons of land-based aircraft and six squadrons operating flying boats. In terms of numbers of aircraft this was almost up to requirements laid down in 1937, though the problem was that there were far too few aircraft which might be considered "modern".

One of the reasons for this difficulty was the dispute between the Air Ministry and the Royal Navy over the ownership of the Fleet Air Arm. Until this was resolved in favour of the Navy in 1937, the Air Ministry was reluctant to provide significant resources to its remaining maritime operation. More simply, priority in new aircraft was being given to Bomber and Fighter Commands.

Major change was proposed towards the end of 1940, with a plan being promoted to place Coastal Command under the control of the Admiralty. Lord Beaverbrook, Minister of Aircraft Production, appears to have been a major proponent of this idea, not least because articles proposing the plan appeared in the *Evening Standard* newspaper which he owned. However, Beaverbrook denied that he had influenced what was written. One of his motives may have been an attempt to embarrass the Air Ministry and, in particular, Sir Archibald Sinclair Bt, Secretary of State for Air, with whom Beaverbrook was frequently at odds.

Lord Trenchard, still a powerful voice at top level, furiously opposed the transfer. There was intensive discussion, with two top-level conferences being held in November 1940 to discuss the issue. Churchill, the Prime Minister, circulated a questionnaire in which he demanded to know what complaints the Admiralty had and how a change would improve operational efficiency and the availability of resources.

Beaverbrook had produced a memorandum putting the case in favour of a change but (demonstrating frequent Beaverbrook failings) it was "lacking in both restraint and sound argument, virtually contributed nothing to the discussion and probably injured rather than promoted the policy of which he was a misguided advocate," according to Captain D. V. Peyton-Ward, a liaison officer between the Royal Navy and Coastal Command.

The outcome, in December 1940, was a decision that Coastal Command should come under the operational control, but not the command, of the Navy.

Many of the activities of the Command and the issues it faced during the Second World War are set out in other entries in this dictionary.

After the war came the inevitable run down of the Command, with the various wartime aircraft types continuing to serve for the time being. Units were sent to the Middle East and took part in the operations to prevent illegal immigrants reaching the new state of Israel.

When the Soviet Union cut off access to Berlin, Coastal Command aircraft participated in the intense and tension-filled air-lift to bring in supplies, maintain the presence of the Western powers in the city and evacuate some civilians. As the Cold War developed, the Command played its part in maintaining the ability of the West to protect itself, particularly in relation to the Atlantic and European waters. Perhaps the best remembered aircraft from that era is the Avro Shackleton long range reconnaissance type, a direct descendant of the Lancaster.

Troops were flown to the Middle East during the Suez Crisis of late 1956. In the early 1960s fishing boats from the Soviet bloc became a nuisance around the UK, both to the comings and goings of British submarines and to the country's fishing fleet. Coastal Command monitored the movements of these vessels and searched for Soviet submarines.

In November 1969 Coastal Command and some other RAF Commands became part of the new Strike Command.

At the same time, the long-running Nimrod era began with the first example of this maritime patrol aircraft reaching No. 236 Operational Conversion Unit on October 2 1969.

The successors to the men and women of Coastal Command took part in the Icelandic "cod wars" of the mid 1970s, the liberation of the Falkland Islands in 1982 (one Nimrod operation involved the dropping of the plans for the re-taking of South Georgia to the County Class destroyer, HMS *Antrim*, this being before the advent of secure Email).

Surveillance and search and rescue sorties were flown during the liberation of Kuwait, the First Gulf War, in 1991, and Nimrods were active in the Balkan theatre. Major rescue tasks included the Fastnet yacht race in 1979 and the explosion on the Piper Alpha oil rig north east of Aberdeen in 1988.

Commanders in Chief of Coastal Command (1936–1948):–

Air Marshal Sir Arthur Longmore	1936
Air Marshal Sir Philip Joubert de la Ferté	1936–1937
Air Marshal Sir Frederick Bowhill	1937–1941
Air Chief Marshal Sir Philip Joubert de la Ferté	1941–1943
Air Marshal Sir John Slessor	1943–1944
Air Chief Marshal Sir Sholto Douglas	1944–1945
Air Marshal Sir Leonard Slatter	1945–1948

The motto of Coastal Command was 'Constant Endeavour'.

Coastal Command and Maritime Air Association – The Association was launched in 1995. Although various old comrades' bodies associated with Coastal Command already existed, "there was felt to be a need for a wider association which would embrace personnel of all ranks who have been or who are currently involved in maritime air operations," according to the Association's website.

The website goes on to state that, "The aim of the CCMAA is to enhance comradeship by maintaining contact between past members of air, sea and ground crews and their modern day successors whilst preserving the traditions of and learning from past and present maritime operations."

A Catalina of No. 202 Squadron pictured off Gibraltar in 1941.

Contact with the Association can be made by Email at: secretary@ ccmaa.org.uk.

Consolidated PBY Catalina – The flying boat, known as the Catalina in the RAF, and sometimes also in the United States forces, was produced by the Consolidated company in the United States, in the 1930s, as a long-range patrol bomber, when a war in the Pacific seemed a distinct possibility. Having gone into production in 1936 this aircraft served in a variety of different roles and was given different names by various users. Examples built in Canada and used by the Royal Canadian Air Force were Catsos, after the then coastal town of Catso in Nova Scotia. Catso ceased to be a separate town in 2012.

Some of the first Catalinas to be received by the RAF had originally been intended for the French Air Force. The type made a major contribution to anti-submarine work and close convoy escorts. It also served in the air sea rescue role.

Other users were the Royal Australian Air Force, Royal New Zealand Air Force and Netherlands Navy. The design was modified for use from airfields.

An account of a Catalina's attack on a U-boat by Andrew Thomas appeared in *Britain at War* (June 2012). The aircraft, a No. 270 Squadron machine, was flying from Bathhurst, Gambia, on January 30 1943 and was skippered by Sergeant John Lort.

"At 13.54 hours they crossed the wake of a surfaced submarine. Sounding the 'action stations' klaxon, Lort hauled his aircraft to port, increased speed and descended to an attack height of between 50 and 100 feet.

"The crew had spotted U-175 on the port bow 45 degrees off the beam – the U-boat was described as being approximately 800 tons, 150–170 feet long and very light grey with a black swastika painted on the conning tower. It was noted that it was armed with one gun mounted forward that was swinging loose ...

"Just one minute after the sighting Lort's navigator logged the first attack – as the post flight report vividly described, 'Aircraft dropped 6 x 250lb Torpex DCs at 25 ft setting and 35 ft intervals. These dropped at an angle of 30 degrees to the port side of the submarine. Nos. 1, 2 and 3 fell short, No. 4 was a very near miss and No. 5 dropped square on the submarine halfway between the conning tower and the stern and No. 6 was another very near miss on the starboard side and just behind the stern. During this time the U-boat took no avoiding action and no effort to man the gun was made.

"After the last DC had gone off, the whole submarine subsided though there was no attempt to crash dive and no bubbles were seen. In the space of seconds the submarine reappeared with the appearance of a 'bounce'.

"As the aircraft flew away after its attack and just as it was turning to port, the air gunner fired three bursts of 15 rounds each. As the aircraft turned to port onto a course of 360 degrees, a subsidence was seen on the water as the submarine sank on an even keel leaving no bubbles with little or no headway on and a patch of oil, 100 ft by 40 ft, was clearly visible."

Helped by a meeting with a supply submarine, *U-175* managed to reach the French port of Lorient. Two months later the submarine, while attacking a convoy, was sunk by the US Coast Guard Cutter *Spencer*. Sergeant Lort was commissioned shortly after the attack related here and, later in 1943, was awarded the DFC.

Consolidated B-24 Liberator – The B-17 Flying Fortress was more famous and considered more glamorous, but the Liberator was produced in much greater numbers and achieved much affection amongst its crews. What would become known as "The Lumbering Lib" first flew on December 29 1939, meeting a US Army Air Corps

One Coastal Command squadron's personnel lined-up in front of an example of "The Lumbering Lib".

requirement for a heavy bomber which was faster than the B-17, had a longer range and a higher operational ceiling.

It was the RAF that bestowed the name "Liberator", which was then adopted by the Americans. As with the Flying Fortress, the Bomber Command hierarchy lacked enthusiasm for the Liberator and so the aircraft eventually became available in considerable numbers to Coastal Command.

The first Coastal Command Liberators arrived at No. 120 Squadron at Nutts Corner, Northern Ireland, in June 1941, giving the RAF the capability of protecting convoys over a much greater distance than before. It was 1943 before the Liberator was a major force in the Command and by the end of that year seven squadrons were equipped with this major addition to its roster of aircraft.

Roles for the Liberator included anti-shipping and anti-submarine operations.

"With the Liberator's ability to patrol for three hours, 1,100 miles out into the Atlantic (compared to the two hours/600–mile endurance of the Sunderland and two hours/600 miles of the Catalina), together with the use of the Azores and Iceland as bases, the Mid-Atlantic Gap was closed and the convoys to west and South Africa were given complete air cover." (*A Brief History of the Royal Air Force*, Ministry of Defence/HMSO).

Convoy Protection – A major duty of Coastal Command was the protection of Allied merchant ships sailing in groups, "convoys", for extra protection. Coastal convoying began almost as soon as the declaration of war had been made. Within a few days the system was applied to ships crossing the Atlantic. Other entries in this Dictionary are also relevant to this fundamental matter, including "Anti-Submarine" and "Atlantic Gap".

"The successful meeting of aircraft and convoy is the responsibility of the navigator. His task and difficulties merit examination. In the

Lockheed Hudsons
of No. 233 Squadron
patrolling over a convoy.

crews of Coastal Command, the navigator is perhaps even more than in
Bomber Command the key man. He is faced with a set of navigational
problems which change literally with the changing wind. His craft is
not moving in an element of which the tides and currents have been
known, charted and tabled for hundreds of years. He has no such
exact information but must rely upon a weather report and forecast.
Changes in the direction and speed of the wind through which he is
to fly cannot be recorded accurately in advance. Temperatures and
pressures vary with every change in the cloud formation. Each flight
is indeed a navigational adventure. The problems of navigation are
much the same when flying over the Atlantic as were those which beset
Columbus when sailing upon its surface ... though the navigator of
aircraft of Coastal Command has drift sights and flame floats to aid

An aerial view of British troops landing on King Red Sector, Gold Beach, on June 6 1944. (*US National Archives*)

him." (From *Coastal Command*, the Air Ministry account of the years 1939 to 1942).

D

D-Day – On June 6 1944, Operation *Overlord*, the invasion of France through Normandy, was launched. This long awaited event became known in the public mind as D-Day and has remained so ever since. In fact, in terms of military planning, operations generally are referred to as beginning at H-Hour on D-Day.

Coastal Command played a considerable part in events on June 6, with Fleet Air Arm, United States Navy and Royal Canadian Air Force units operating within Nos. 16 and 19 Groups of the Command.

According to the Ministry of Defence website, "The two Groups were given separate areas of responsibility. 19 Group, based in South West England, were to operate in the South West Approaches and 16 Group were to protect the Channel and the Thames Estuary."

Decorations – The Victoria Cross, George Cross and George Medal are covered elsewhere in this Dictionary. The other gallantry decorations normally available to Coastal Command aircrew during the Second World War were, for officers, the Distinguished Service Order (DSO), with the Distinguished Flying Cross (DFC) and the Air Force Cross (AFC) for officers and Warrant Officers. Other ranks awards were the Conspicuous Gallantry Medal (CGM), the Distinguished Flying Medal (DFM) and the Air Force Medal (AFM).

The DSO was instituted in 1886 and involved admission to an order; until the early years of the First World War some awards were made for services not performed under fire. At its institution it was available to officers in both the Royal Navy and Army – A revised Royal Warrant approved on April 1 1918 extended the award to the newly-formed RAF. As a gallantry decoration the DSO ranked immediately below the VC.

At the beginning of the Second World War there was no decoration for RAF other ranks at the second level, that is between the VC and the DFM, unlike the Royal Navy which had the CGM and the Army which had the Distinguished Conduct Medal (DCM). To make good this deficiency a Royal Warrant of November 10 1942 extended the CGM to other ranks of the Army and the RAF for deeds, "whilst flying in active operations against the enemy".

The DFC was instituted by a Royal Warrant of June 3 1918, just over two months after the formation of the RAF. This warrant also established the DFM, AFC and AFM. The AFC and the AFM were awarded for courage or devotion to duty while flying, but not during operations against the enemy.

The DFC and the DFM were awarded for an act or acts of valour, courage or devotion to duty performed, "whilst flying in active operations against the enemy". The awards were equivalent to the Royal Navy's Distinguished Service Cross (DSC) and Distinguished Service Medal (DSM) and the Army's Military Cross (MC) and Military Medal (MM). Other ranks sometimes received the British Empire Medal (BEM) for gallant acts.

Some RAF personnel who performed gallant acts, not in the air, received Royal Navy and Army awards.

Following a fundamental review of the system for gallantry awards, instigated by the then Prime Minister, John Major, in 1993, the DFM and AFM, together with the other service equivalents, ceased to be awarded and all ranks became eligible for those previously awarded only to officers and warrant officers.

In the 1993 changes the second level awards of all three services were replaced by the Conspicuous Gallantry Cross (CGC), with the DSO reserved for outstanding leadership and service on military operations.

De-gaussing – A process of reducing or largely eliminating a magnetic field.

At the outbreak of war both Britain and Germany were developing magnetic mines, designed to explode when a ship was in the vicinity. The Germans deployed such mines first and dealing with them was dangerous work for Royal Navy minesweepers.

Hasty action was required. Ships were de-gaussed – treated to reduce the likelihood of them triggering a magnetic mine – and some Vickers Wellingtons were fitted with ungainly looking "de-gaussing rings". The aircraft were flown over areas believed to contain German mines and the ring created a magnetic field with enough force to explode the mines. For security reasons these were known as DWI Wellingtons, the letters standing for "Directional Wireless Installation".

A Vickers Wellington fitted with a de-gaussing ring.

On January 8 1940, a Wellington, equipped with a de-gaussing ring, operating from Manston, as part of No. 1 General Reconnaissance Unit (within No. 16 Group), flew a sortie over the Thames estuary and succeeded in detonating a mine without damage to the aircraft. However, this was clearly another dangerous way of dealing with magnetic mines and better methods were soon developed.

de Havilland Mosquito – When, before the war, de Havilland put forward the concept that became the Mosquito, it was received without enthusiasm by many decision makers. The proposed all-wood construction was certainly a factor in this attitude. Wood came more into favour when it was realised, after hostilities started, that one impact of the German U-boat campaign was to create a shortage of light alloy.

An Air Ministry order was placed in 1940, but progress was still slow. In 1941 the first "Mossie" or "Wooden Wonder" to fly an operational sortie was one of those adapted for PR work. Mosquitos went on to serve the RAF (and the RAAF, RNZAF, RCAF, SAAF and USAAF) in a wide variety of combat and other roles. In Coastal Command the type was an effective weapon deployed by the Strike Wings.

The Mosquito carried a crew of two (slimness was an asset when escaping hurriedly through the hatch in the floor). Nearly 8,000 were built including construction in Australia and Canada. Varieties of the Rolls Royce Merlin engine were fitted. Speed was a Mosquito attribute and so was the ability to take punishment.

Well into the post-war world the RAF continued to make use of the versatility of the Mosquito.

Douglas, Marshal of the Royal Air Force Lord Douglas of Kirtleside (1893–1969) – (William) Sholto Douglas was born in Oxford. His father was the Secretary of the Church of England Temperance Society, however Douglas senior left the priesthood, the marriage was dissolved and he went on to have a colourful personal and professional life. The young Sholto was brought up by his mother. He attended a number of schools, culminating in five years at Tonbridge, from where he gained a classical scholarship to Lincoln College, Oxford. His activities at the university included membership of the artillery section of the OTC.

Within two weeks of the outbreak of the Great War, Douglas, having abandoned his university course, was commissioned in the Royal Field Artillery and soon went to France. Later in 1914 he transferred to the Royal Flying Corps, serving as an observer with No. 2 Squadron. In 1915 he trained as a pilot. He went to No. 8 Squadron on the Western Front and earned the MC. Despite this recognition, some commentators, in later years, drew attention to a tendency they felt Douglas had to exaggerate his combat achievements and the speed of his advancement.

His next move, as a Major in May 1916, was to Stirling in Scotland, where he commanded the newly-formed No. 43 Squadron, later to achieve fame as "The Fighting Cocks". The squadron moved south to Netheravon and then Northolt, before going across the Channel to St Omer in January 1917. Later in the year Douglas took command of No. 84 Squadron, which was being equipped with the SE5a fighter. By the end of the fighting in 1918 he had reached the rank of Lieutenant Colonel in the new RAF and a DFC was gazetted in 1919. In that year Douglas left the RAF. He tried various jobs, including as a pilot with Handley Page, but, by his own account, he was at a loose end at the beginning of 1920 and considering a job opportunity in India, when a chance meeting with Air Chief Marshal Sir Hugh Trenchard led to a return to the RAF, as a Squadron Leader and with a staff post at No. 1 Group at Kenley.

Douglas went on to attend the RAF Staff College, Andover and the Imperial Defence College in London. He served in the Middle East and then went back to the Imperial Defence College as an instructor. From 1936 he was at the Air Ministry as Director of Staff Duties and then as Assistant Chief of the Air Staff, responsible for weapons and equipment during the build-up to war and the early days of the conflict. From January 1938 he held the rank of Air Vice-Marshal.

In November 1940, elevated to Air Marshal, he replaced Air Chief Marshal Sir Hugh Dowding (who had been his CO at No. 1 Group twenty years previously) as Air Officer Commanding in Chief, Fighter Command. This was a deeply-controversial appointment and the heated debate over the manner of Dowding's removal and the part that Douglas may have played in it continues to resound in the twenty-first century. Douglas's time at Fighter Command would generate further controversy. Following the offensive doctrine of his old mentor, Trenchard, Douglas presided over the fighter sweeps to the Continent during 1941, during which many of the veterans of the Battle of Britain were killed or taken prisoner.

From December 1942 Sholto Douglas, now an Air Chief Marshal, was head of RAF Middle East. He might have gone on to be Allied

Commander, South East Asia, but senior Americans were unimpressed with both his record and his manner and a veto on the appointment was the result. A further snub followed when Lieutenant General Ira C. Eaker was made Commander in Chief of the new Mediterranean Allied Air Forces, with Douglas as his intended deputy.

A difficult situation was resolved by the appointment of Douglas to Coastal Command at the beginning of 1944, with Operation *Overlord*, the planned invasion of western Europe, fast approaching.

In August 1945 Douglas took up the appointment of head of British Air Forces of Occupation in Germany and five months later he became one of only two RAF officers in its history (the other was Sir Arthur Harris) to reach the rank of Marshal of the Royal Air Force without serving as Chief of the Air Staff. In May 1946, he became Commander in Chief of British forces in Germany, as well as Military Governor of the British zone. Douglas would complain that Field Marshal Montgomery, his predecessor, made almost no effort to brief him at the handover and was elsewhere in Germany when Douglas arrived to take over.

Technically Marshals of the Royal Air Force never retire, but Douglas ceased to hold any appointment in November 1947. In February 1948 he was raised to the Peerage as Lord Douglas of Kirtleside. The River Kirtle flows into the Solway Firth and Douglas forebears came from that area of Scotland. Douglas became a director of BOAC and then Chairman of BEA.

Dynamo, Operation – The German "Blitzkrieg" (lightning war) through France, Belgium, The Netherlands and Luxembourg, began on May 10 1940. Despite much bitter and often heroic fighting, hundreds of thousands of British and French troops found themselves retreating on the port of Dunkirk and the immediate area. Operation *Dynamo*, to bring as many of these men as possible back to England, was launched on May 26. Dynamo was under the control of Vice

Admiral Bertram Ramsay, Vice Admiral Dover, with his headquarters at Dover Castle.

The original hope for Operation *Dynamo* was that 48,000 men might be rescued from the beaches across the Channel. In the event, when the operation drew to a close on June 4, with German troops having entered Dunkirk, the total number of Allied soldiers brought back was 338,226. This had been achieved by the use of Royal Navy vessels, but also by the band of "Little Ships", often crewed by civilian men and women, from teenagers to the elderly. They carried out their work under constant German gunfire and air attack and many were lost. Thus the terms "Miracle of Dunkirk" and "Dunkirk Spirit" entered the language.

Despite claims by the Army at the time that the RAF had mounted insufficient effort, Coastal Command and the other main RAF Commands all flew many sorties in defence of the beaches. There were also RAF launches from Calshot, under the command of Pilot Officer C. Collings, among the Little Ships.

A vivid and detailed account of the Dunkirk evacuation from a maritime prospective was given in the book *Dunkirk*, by A. D. Divine, published in 1945. Writing of the events of June 1, the author noted that, "Fighter Command, Coastal Command and the Fleet Air Arm worked desperately throughout the day (but) there were simply not enough planes at any time to give continuous cover to the channels of approach, to the roadsteads, to the beaches and to the hard pressed men of the perimeter … Three Anson reconnaissance aircraft of Coastal Command engaged nine Messerschmitt fighters, at one period of the day, flying almost at water level." Three Hudsons found "a patch of sky black with Jerrys".

The Anson crews claimed two destroyed and two possibly destroyed. The Hudson men claimed three destroyed and two possibly destroyed.

From Air Ministry signal, June 3 1940:

"This signals [*sic*] confirms arrangements made by telephone for providing fighter protection for Dunkirk and shipping in evacuation over the period 19.30 hours 3rd June to 08.00 hours 4th June.

"Coastal Command to provide protection for shipping between Dover and Dunkirk during period 19.30 hours till dark.

"Fighter Command to maintain continuous patrol – strength one Blenheim fighter – over Dunkirk area during hours of darkness.

"Fighter protection to be provided over Dunkirk area and shipping in the channel from 04.30 hours to 08.00 hours 4th June, protection to be provided by Fighter Command followed by Coastal Command."

In the House of Commons on June 4 Winston Churchill made his, "We shall fight on the beaches" speech in which he also said:

"This was a great trial of strength between the British and German air forces. Can you conceive a greater objective for the Germans in the air than to make evacuation from these beaches impossible, and to sink all these ships which were displayed, almost to the extent of thousands?

A Hudson of No. 220 Squadron over the Dunkirk beaches during Operation *Dynamo*.

Could there have been an objective of greater military importance and significance for the whole purpose of the war than this? They tried hard, and they were beaten back; they were frustrated in their task. We got the Army away; and they have paid fourfold for any losses which they have inflicted."

According to the Air Historical Branch narrative account, Coastal Command losses during Operation *Dynamo* included fourteen Blenheims and twenty Hudsons. RAF personnel killed, missing or wounded in all commands amounted to 1382, of which 915 were aircrew and 534 of those were pilots.

Although the events at Dunkirk at this time are the best remembered, evacuations also took place from a number of other French ports.

F

Fish – Standard everyday name for a torpedo.

Flak Ship – Term used in the Coastal Command Strike Wings when referring to heavily-armed converted trawlers deployed by the Germans to protect convoys against aerial attack. In official circles they were "trawler-type auxiliaries", while the enemy referred to them as "Vorpostenboot". A bigger threat to the RAF was posed by former merchant vessels, also heavily armed, given the designation, "Sperrbrecher".

Focke-Wulf Fw 200 Condor – A Luftwaffe aircraft that became a particular foe of Coastal Command. It was a four-engine design, developed originally for use as a commercial airliner, but a version for maritime reconnaissance and the bombing of shipping was then produced. In addition, the Luftwaffe also used the type for transport purposes. One of the Condor's attributes was its relative speed for a large aircraft and compared with some of the Coastal Command types expected to deal with it.

A Condor which was downed by a Hudson.

G

George Cross – This decoration, GC for short, was instituted in September 1940 by King George VI. It superseded the Medal of the Order of the British Empire for Gallantry, usually known as the Empire Gallantry Medal (EGM). The award of the George Cross was intended to recognise acts by civilians or deeds of military personnel which, broadly, were not directly in the presence of the enemy, though there has been much debate over the years about the definition of the word "presence" in this context.

"It is ordained that the persons eligible for the Decoration of the Cross shall be Our faithful subjects and persons under Our protection in civil life, male and female; persons of any rank in the Naval, Military or Air Forces of Our United Kingdom or persons within and members of the Naval, Military or Air Forces of Our Dominions or Government whereof … The Cross is intended primarily for civilians and award in Our military services is to be confined to actions for which purely military Honours are not normally granted. … It is ordained that the Cross shall be awarded only for acts of the greatest heroism or of the most conspicuous courage in circumstances of extreme danger, and that the Cross may be awarded posthumously." (From the Royal Warrant instituting the George Cross, dated September 24 1940).

In 1941 holders of the EGM and relatives of holders who had died since September 3 1939 were required to exchange their decoration for the GC. In 1971 living holders of the Albert Medal and the Edward Medal were invited to do the same.

One person serving in Coastal Command who was awarded the GC, albeit posthumously, was Flying Officer Roderick Borden Gray, RCAF of No. 172 Squadron.

The citation for Flying Officer Gray's award appeared in *The London Gazette* on March 12 1945. It recorded that:

"One night in August, 1944, this officer was the navigator of a Wellington aircraft which was shot down into the Atlantic by a U-boat. Flying Officer Gray and three other members of the crew managed to extricate themselves from the aircraft. Despite a severe wound in the leg, Flying Officer Gray succeeded in inflating his own dinghy, and assisted into it his Captain, who had also been wounded. Cries were shortly heard from another member of the crew, who had broken his arm; Flying Officer Gray helped him also into the dinghy. Although suffering intense pain, Flying Officer Gray refused to get into the dinghy, knowing that it could not hold more than two persons and for some hours he hung on to its side, aided by one of its occupants and by the fourth member of the crew. In spite of increasing pain and exhaustion, he steadfastly refused to endanger his comrades by entering the dinghy, and eventually lost consciousness and died. When it became light his companions, realising that he was dead, were forced to let his body sink. Flying Officer Gray displayed magnificent courage and unselfish heroism, thus enabling the lives of his comrades to be saved."

At the same time as the institution of the GC the George Medal (GM) for wider distribution was announced. A Coastal Command recipient of this decoration was Wing Commander Jack Davenport, Officer Commanding No. 455 Squadron, RAAF.

On September 9 1944, the port engine of a Beaufighter failed while returning to Langham from a reconnaissance of the Dutch coast. The aircraft ground-looped on landing at base and caught fire. The navigator, Flying Officer Kenneth Dempsey, leapt through the flames and got clear, but Flying Officer Bill Stanley, the pilot, was trapped. Wing Commander Davenport ran to the scene from the control tower and, having ordered all others present to keep away, braved the flames and exploding ammunition, climbed on to a wing, released the hatch and leaned into the cockpit. The main plane collapsed, but Davenport eventually managed to pull the badly-burned pilot to safety, having suffered burns himself. Stanley survived, insisting on reporting the results of the reconnaissance, before being taken to hospital.

One onlooker described the rescue as, "the most amazing thing I have seen in this war". A recommendation for the award of the George Medal was submitted by the Officer Commanding, Langham, Group Captain Arthur Clouston, and was accepted. It was one of twenty awards of the GM made to members of the RAAF during the Second World War.

In passing, it is worth noting that the idea often put forward that the Victoria Cross (see separate entry) at the time the GC was instituted, was only open to military personnel, was not strictly true. Such awards were allowed under certain circumstances.

For instance, the VC warrant of February 5 1931 refers to the eligibility of, "Matrons, Sisters, Nurses and the staff of the nursing services and other services pertaining to hospitals and nursing, and civilians of either sex serving regularly or temporarily under the orders, direction or supervision" of any of the military forces mentioned in the warrant.

However, since 1940, there have been occasions when civilians performing valorous acts, while under military command and in the presence of the enemy, have been awarded the GC (for example, Captain Dudley Mason, Master of the tanker SS *Ohio*, which reached Malta in August 1942, as a survivor of the *Pedestal* convoy, despite constant enemy attack and severe damage) and this had clearly become the policy.

See also entries for Victoria Cross and Women's Auxiliary Air Force.

Gibraltar – The small British territory at the southern end of the Iberian Peninsula, was captured from the Spanish in 1704 during the War of Spanish Succession. Initially this was on behalf of a claimant to the Spanish throne, but in 1713 the Treaty of Utrecht ceded Gibraltar to Britain, "in perpetuity". British possession of the territory remains highly controversial with Spain today. Gibraltar's military importance stemmed mainly from its position at the entrance to the Mediterranean.

From 1941 Coastal Command squadrons were based at Gibraltar. The intention was to give protection to convoys sailing to Gibraltar and to Freetown in west Africa, as well as those sailing onwards to Malta. There was also the intention to provide a presence in the western Mediterranean (supporting the Royal Navy's Force H), and along the coasts of Spain and Portugal, including the countering of hostile acts by French forces.

Early squadrons at "Gib" included No. 233 with Hudsons and No. 202 with Catalinas and, later, Sunderlands.

Another part of the service to have a heavy presence in Gib was the RAF Regiment, formed in 1942. To this day personnel serving in the

Regiment are known as "Rock Apes" to the rest of the RAF – "Rock Ape" being a popular name for the Barbary Macaque monkey found on Gibraltar.

Gloster Gladiator – The Gladiator was the last biplane fighter employed by the RAF (also the first with an enclosed cockpit) and was already obsolete when it entered service in 1937, initially with No. 72 Squadron. Nonetheless, the Gladiator is well remembered for various theatres in which it saw action during the Second World War, including the Norwegian campaign and the siege of Malta.

The Gladiator was a development of the Gloster Gauntlet. There was a Sea Gladiator variant for the Royal Navy and the type was exported to a considerable number of countries including Belgium, China, Norway, South Africa, Portugal and Greece.

In Coastal Command, the Gladiator was adapted for meteorological flights.

Groups – Groups rank in the RAF command structure below Commands and above Squadrons.

In early 1943 the Coastal Command order of battle featured four groups:-

No. 15 Group (headquarters at Liverpool) and operating, in particular, from, Aldergrove, Ballykelly (County Londonderry), Lough Erne, Oban, Bowmore (on the island of Islay) and Benbecula (North Uist). The Group was disbanded on August 1 1945.

No. 16 Group (Chatham), Bircham Newton (Norfolk), Docking (Norfolk), North Coates and Thorney Island.

No. 18 Group (Pitreavie Castle, Fife), Leuchars, Woodhaven (Fife), Sullom Voe (Shetland) and Wick.

No. 19 Group (Plymouth), Beaulieu, Chivenor, Talbenny (Pembrokeshire), Dale (Pembrokeshire), St Eval, Predannack, Mount Batten (Plymouth Sound), Pembroke Dock, Hamworthy Junction (Poole Harbour) and Holmesley South (Hampshire).

At that time, the Fleet Air Arm's Nos. 833 and 836 Squadrons were on loan to Coastal Command and were based at Thorney Island.

H

Handley Page Halifax – The Halifax entered RAF service, with No. 35 Squadron in Bomber Command, towards the end of 1940, having first flown in late 1939. As the bomber offensive gathered pace from 1942, this four-engine type proved to be one of the Command's major weapons, though outshone in fame and public affection by the Lancaster. However, the Halifax was an aircraft in which the crew stood a good chance of getting home, even with considerable damage. It came to be referred to in the RAF as the "Halibag".

As first flown at Bicester, Oxfordshire on October 25 1939, the Halifax had four Rolls Royce Merlin engines and provision for a crew of seven.

Despite the demands of the bomber offensive, the Halifax was made available to Coastal Command and was modified for its use. Halifaxes equipped nine squadrons and contributed considerably to anti-submarine, anti-shipping and meteorological duties.

Handley Page Hampden – The Hampden was a result of an Air Ministry specification of 1932, calling for a twin-engine bomber, which also led to the very different Vickers Wellington.

In its Bomber Command form the Hampden was equipped with Bristol Pegasus radial piston engines and normally carried a crew of four and up to 4,000lb of bombs. It had a maximum speed of just over 250 mph. There were twin forward firing 0.303in machine-guns and

The prototype Handley Page Hampden, K 4240, first flew, without armament, on June 21 1936.

further guns of the same type in ventral and dorsal positions. This armament was insufficient to counter Messerschmitt Bf 109s in daylight, a problem which Coastal Command would find represented a severe drawback. The first flight by a Hampden was in 1936.

In Bomber Command Hampden crews performed gallantly in the early years of the war, but the type was withdrawn from front line service as four-engine "heavies" became available.

Coastal Command uses of the Hampden included meteorological flights, anti-shipping operations and as a torpedo bomber. The latter role was one of its least successful manifestations, offering one of many examples of Coastal Command adapting aircraft designed for other purposes to meet the tasks allotted to the Command.

I

Iceland – This island is situated where the Atlantic and Arctic oceans meet, with an area of about 320,000 square miles and a sparse population. In the Second World War it was a much used staging post between North America and Europe.

Hudsons over Iceland.

In August 1940 No. 30 Wing, controlled by No. 18 Group, arrived in Iceland. Seven months later AHQ Iceland was established and No. 100 Wing started to control flying boat operations in the harbour at Reykjavik. Activities ceased at the end of the war.

On August 27 1941, a Hudson of No. 269 Squadron, operating from Iceland and flown by Squadron Leader J. H. Thompson, depth charged *U-570* and caused it to surrender. The submarine was badly damaged, one result of which was that the crew believed that chlorine gas (used by the Germans as a weapon against British troops in the First World War) was leaking from the battery compartment. After a delay caused by various factors including the need to get British ships to the scene and heavy seas, a Royal Navy boarding party went aboard the vessel and it was towed to Iceland. *U-570* later became HMS *Graph*, thereby seeing operational service for both sides. Coastal Command flew from Iceland in support of the Arctic convoys.

The Type VIIC U-boat *U-570* pictured during and following its surrender to the No. 269 Squadron Coastal Command Lockheed Hudson flown by Squadron Leader James H. Thompson on August 27 1941. Following the surrender of *U-570*, Allied surface vessels soon arrived on the scene – one of which can be seen here.

Ireland (relations with) – The present Republic of Ireland came into existence as the Irish Free State, in 1922, with Dublin as the capital. It comprised twenty-six of the thirty-two Irish counties and ceased to be a part of the UK. Until 1948 Ireland remained a member of the British Commonwealth. The other six counties formed Northern Ireland, Belfast being the chief city, which remained in the UK.

In 1938 Britain handed back to Ireland the three naval bases it had retained – at Queenstown (Cork Harbour, now Cobh), Lough Swilly in Donegal and Berehaven (Bantry Bay).

The Dublin government declared the country neutral on September 4 1939, the day after Britain and France declared war on Germany. In a complex situation, the Irish authorities took the view that there could be no military support for Britain while Ireland remained partitioned. However, economic relations with Britain continued to be vital to Ireland and "neutrality" was interpreted in different ways.

Many Irish citizens served in the British forces and many more worked in civilian jobs in Britain. Intelligence and weather information was passed from Ireland to Britain. Several hundred members of the IRA were also interned as a gesture to Britain.

The Irish Air Corps had been purchasing British aircraft before the war and, for example, Miles Magister training aircraft were supplied into 1940. Three Hurricanes that forced-landed in Ireland during 1940 and 1941 were taken on charge by the Air Corps and payment for them was made to Britain, with spares travelling in the opposite direction. Britain sold more Hurricanes to Ireland later in the war and at least one RAF pilot was attached to the Irish Air Corps as an instructor.

RAF aircrew who landed inadvertently in Ireland on training flights were repatriated, however those who came down during operational flights in the first half of the war were interned. All had been released by the end of 1943. There was a "diplomatic incident" when an American national serving in the RAF escaped back to Northern Ireland. He was returned to the south for a brief period. USAAF personnel were not interned, whereas German aircrew were held for the duration. About 200 British aircraft came down in Ireland during the war.

RAF flights were allowed to cross Irish air space in the northwest of the country to reach the Atlantic. This included Coastal Command flying boats operating from RAF Castle Archdale in Northern Ireland.

J

Joubert de la Ferte Bennet, Air Chief Marshal Sir Philip (1887–1965) – Joubert was born in India of partly French descent. His father was a member of the Indian Medical Service. Joubert attended Harrow School, then was a student at the Royal Military Academy, Woolwich, subsequently being commissioned in the Royal Field Artillery.

In 1912 Joubert took flying lessons at Brooklands aerodrome, Surrey, at his own expense. He gained Royal Aero Club certificate No. 280. He enrolled on a course at the Central Flying School and joined the Royal Flying Corps in 1913. In 1914 he went to France with No. 3 Squadron and, shortly afterwards, took part in the first aerial reconnaissance over enemy lines. He had a spell in England and then returned to France, as a Temporary Major, to command No. 15 Squadron, moving on to command No. 1 Squadron.

Joubert left France suffering from trench foot. He later commanded a Wing in Egypt and was awarded the DSO. He led a Wing in Italy and then commanded the RFC in the country.

After the war Joubert was given a permanent commission in the RAF, with the rank of Wing Commander. He went on to hold staff appointments at the Air Ministry and became the first RAF instructor at the Imperial Defence College. He was Commandant of the RAF Staff College.

As an Air Vice-Marshal in 1934, Joubert was appointed to command Fighting Area of Great Britain. Promoted Air Marshal, he undertook his first spell in command of Coastal Command and then became Air Officer Commanding in India, where he would experience some of the frustration at needs not being recognised, which would be a feature of his later service with Coastal Command. He was appointed KCB in 1938.

Returning to the UK he was, for a time, Assistant Chief of the Air Staff, particularly concerned with the development of radar. He was promoted Air Chief Marshal in 1941 and returned to Coastal Command.

Air Chief Marshal Sir Philip Joubert de la Ferte Bennet.

In his second spell in charge of Coastal Command Joubert made himself unpopular at the top level for his persistence in arguing that the Command needed more resources so that it could prosecute the anti-submarine campaign. Between the time when it was announced that he was leaving and the actual date, the Casablanca conference of political leaders took place, when it was decided that for Britain and the United States, the defeat of the U-boats would be given priority in 1943.

Joubert was appointed Inspector General of the RAF and retired later in 1943, but was very quickly recalled to join the staff of South East Asia Command. He retired again in October 1945 and, as a civilian, was Director of Public Relations at the Air Ministry.

"[Joubert] belongs to a familiar category of unfortunates: those officers, in different services and in different wars, who preside over bad times, weather the worst storms, but do not remain in command when the change of fortune comes and the reward of strain and effort can be collected." (John Terraine in *The Right of the Line*).

K

Kipper Fleet – Nickname applied to Coastal Command by the rest of the RAF. To RAF personnel the Royal Navy is often, "The Grey Funnel Line".

L

Leigh Light – Powerful searchlight fitted to Coastal Command aircraft from 1942, as an aid to attacking surfaced U-boats at night, often while they were recharging their batteries. Radar was used to detect the submarine and arrive in its vicinity. The Leigh Light was switched on for the final approach. The device proved highly successful.

The Leigh Light was named after its creator, Wing Commander Humphrey de Verd Leigh (1897–1980) who had served in the Royal

Naval Air Service and the RAF, as a pilot, in the First World War. Having re-joined the RAF on the outbreak of the Second World War, he undertook personnel and staff roles. His invention was developed on his own initiative, after he had talked to aircrew about their problems, and it quickly received enthusiastic support from the staff at Coastal Command.

However, there were setbacks, for example when Sir Philip Joubert took over Coastal Command for the second time. At the Air Ministry Joubert had worked with the scientist and RAF officer, William Helmore, on the development of the Helmore Light, or Turbinlite, intended initially to be used by Fighter Command to illuminate German bombers at night. Joubert considered the Leigh Light merely a variant of the Helmore.

Joubert later wrote, "When I first took over at Coastal Command having been so closely associated with the Helmore Light I thought it might be given a general application by being used against U-boats as well. I thought that its wide beam and great illuminating power would be valuable. I therefore gave instruction that … Leigh was to return to his duties as Assistant Personnel Officer. After some two months I found, as I do not mind admitting, that I had made a mistake. I found out that the Helmore Light was unnecessarily brilliant for use against U-boats and otherwise unsuitable. I then came to the conclusion that Leigh's light was preferable for use against the U-boat and decided to drop the Helmore Light and concentrate on the Leigh Light." A refinement in the Leigh Light came when the beam width was increased.

According to Sir Maurice Dean, Leigh Light aircraft attacked 218 U-boats at night and carried out 206 attacks on enemy shipping. The same source gives twenty-seven as the number of U-boats sunk, where the attack involved the use of Leigh Lights, with thirty-one damaged.

Leuchars – The airfield at Leuchars in Fife was associated with aviation from the very early days. Before the First World War the Royal Engineers had established a training camp there for balloon personnel.

On the day war broke out, September 3 1939, Wing Commander E A Hodgson, CO of
No. 224 Squadron was pictured at Leuchars inspecting fuzes of 112lb bombs, before they
were loaded on to Hudsons.

Aircraft also arrived and the site became a base for the training of spotting crews who provided information to Royal Navy capital ships. RAF Leuchars was officially established in 1920.

For a time in the 1930s No. 1 Flying Training School was at Leuchars. From 1938 Coastal Command took over. Nos. 224 and 233 Squadrons, both operating Anson Mk Is, officially took up residence on 1 September. The station's aircraft were quick to see action after the outbreak of the Second World War, but they spent much of their time on the routine of maritime patrols. It was a No. 224 Squadron aircraft that spotted the German prison ship *Altmark* (see separate entry) in February 1940. By that time the squadron was using Hudsons.

A change after the Second World War, was "ownership" by Fighter Command and the appearance of jet fighters, starting with the Meteor.

In 2015 Leuchars became an Army base.

Lindholme Gear – This was a long-serving survival system, named after RAF Lindholme in Yorkshire and designed to be dropped to downed aircrew in water. It was first used in the spring of 1941, and featured a number of cylinder-like containers, held together by rope. The containers held an inflatable dinghy, food, clothing and other survival equipment.

Lockheed Hudson – The Hudson was an aircraft designed pre-war with both military and civilian use in mind. It was a leap forward for the Lockheed Corporation when the RAF placed a major order and the Hudson was much used by Coastal Command in bombing, reconnaissance and air sea rescue roles. For the latter task Hudsons were adapted to carry a lifeboat to be dropped to airmen in the sea. Hudsons also served in the RAF in training and transport duties and undertook clandestine operations to occupied Europe and in the Far East.

Other operators included the RAAF, RCAF, RNZAF and USAAF.

A Lockheed Hudson in flight.

There was a tendency for Hudsons to catch fire as a result of any significant crash, a problem attributed to the design of the petrol system. Weight had been saved by using the metal skin of the wing as petrol tanks, with the wing root made petrol-tight. The engine exhaust pipes were nearby and leaks of fuel occurred as soon as the riveting on the wing surfaces broke. The large battery carried was another factor.

"The second pilot ran back to man the side gun of the Hudson. I went all out on the throttle and at 1,100ft began to dive. Four hundred yards away I was wondering who would fire first. At that moment the German and I began firing simultaneously, but my front guns didn't seem to be doing him any damage … I brought my Hudson still lower and got into position 200 yards away to give my rear gunner a chance. He took it beautifully and promptly. I could see the tracer bullets from his tail gun whipping into the Focke-Wulf's two port engines and into its fuselage about mid-wing."

The above is part of the description given by a Coastal Command pilot, on the BBC, of shooting down a Luftwaffe Condor as it was

The cockpit of a No. 224 Squadron Hudson.

about to attack a convoy. During 1941 more than 280 RAF and WAAF personnel broadcast on their experiences anonymously.

"On 10 January 1940 Flying Officer McLaren, with Pilot Officer Evans as second pilot, attacked a Heinkel III. After two front gun attacks its undercarriage dropped half down and the rear guns were silenced. After all the front gun ammunition had been shot away he climbed above the Heinkel and dropped two 250 pound anti-submarine bombs on it from about 100 feet above but these both missed. They then attacked with several free gun beam and quarter attacks until the turret hydraulic system failed, making it impossible to train the guns, and the action had to be broken off.

"The Hudson expended 1,500 rounds of ammunition and was hit by eleven bullets from the Heinkel." (Extract from Operations Record Book of No. 233 Squadron).

Longmore, Air Chief Marshal Sir Arthur Murray (1885–1970) –
Longmore was the first Air Officer Commanding in Chief of Coastal
Command, and had also had a spell commanding its predecessor,
Coastal Area. He therefore found himself a key figure in the struggle
to ready the Command for war with Germany.

Longmore was born in Australia, the son of a railway stationmaster,
but lived in England from the age of seven with his mother. He became
a naval cadet on the training ship *Britannia* in 1900 and received a
commission in the Royal Navy in 1904. He became a very early naval
aviator, gaining his pilot's certificate from the Royal Aero Club (No. 72)
in 1910. For a time, he was an instructor at the Central Flying School.

Air Chief Marshal Sir Arthur
Longmore, photographed
whilst serving as Air Officer
Commanding-in-Chief Middle
East Command.

After the outbreak of war Longmore saw action in France, forming and commanding No. 1 Squadron, Royal Naval Air Service. He went back to sea in HMS *Tiger*, though he had not wished to stop flying, and was in the ship at the Battle of Jutland, where he considered that an opportunity was lost to use aircraft, especially in a reconnaissance role.

Longmore was later in Malta on the staff of the Commander in Chief Mediterranean. As a Lieutenant Colonel in the new RAF he led a successful campaign against U-boat bases in the Mediterranean and was appointed DSO in 1919.

During the 1920s Longmore's postings included a staff job in Iraq and a period at the Air Ministry. He became Commandant of the RAF College, Cranwell, in 1929 and stayed in a post he found particularly congenial until 1932.

Longmore commanded Inland Area, became Commandant of the Imperial Defence College and was appointed KCB in 1935. He led Training Command in 1939–1940 when the establishment of the Empire Air Training Scheme was a key issue on his desk. Then he went to the Middle East as Air Officer Commanding in Chief. After disagreement with Winston Churchill Longmore returned to the UK and was made Inspector General of the RAF. He retired from the service in 1942. He was unsuccessful when, as a Conservative, he contested a by-election at Grantham. Longmore then returned to the RAF and became a member of the post-hostilities planning committee. He retired again in 1944 and gave much service to the Imperial War Graves Commission.

The Civil Servant Sir Maurice Dean found Longmore, "intelligent, polished, highly competent and imperturbable."

One of Longmore's sons, Wing Commander Richard Maitland Longmore, was killed in action while serving with Coastal Command. On October 4 1943, as Officer Commanding No. 120 Squadron, he was skipper of a Liberator that attacked the U-boat, *U 539*. The aircraft was shot down and there were no survivors.

See also entry for Squadrons.

M

Memorials – Examples of the ways in which those who served in Coastal Command are remembered include:

A memorial, commemorating Coastal Command aircrew who lost their lives in the Second World War, stands close to the Scottish Seabird Centre at North Berwick looking out to the Bass Rock.

At St Eval in Cornwall the words on the memorial are:-

RAF St Eval 1939–1959
In Memory of those who served and the 974 gallant aircrew who lost their lives. Also the 22 airmen and WAAFs who were killed in bombing raids.

Unveiled this day 10th April 2005 by Wing Commander Keith Cowieson RAF and dedicated by the Reverend G R Muttram MA, 206 Squadron 1952–1956 and the Reverend T. Wright BSc, Chaplain RAF St Mawgan.
WE WILL REMEMBER THEM

Erected by RAF St Eval Coastal Command Association

The RAF Pembroke Dock memorial window is now kept by the RAF Museum, Hendon. It incorporates the badges of all the squadrons that were stationed at Pembroke Dock during the Second World War – Nos. 119, 201, 209, 210, 228, 240, 320 and 321 Squadrons (RAF), 10 and 461 Squadrons (RAAF), 422 (RCAF) and VP-63 of the United States Navy, as well as marine craft and RAF Pembroke Dock.

A replica was unveiled at Pembroke Dock in 1995 by Flight Lieutenant John Cruickshank VC. It was later kept at Pembroke Dock Library.

The wording on this memorial reads, "In proud and grateful memory of the officers and men who gave their lives whilst serving on this station in the cause of freedom, 1939–1945."

The St Eval window. (*Courtesy of Dr Mark Charter*)

A memorial at Bircham Newton was unveiled in 2006. The associations connected with Nos. 206 and 221 Squadrons were among a range of organisations that supported the RAF Bircham Newton Memorial Project in achieving this objective. The latter organisation also erected a memorial in 2007 at the former Bircham Newton satellite of Docking.

On the Banff to Portsoy road stands the memorial to the RAF Banff Strike Wing, containing the inscription:

"This memorial commemorates the men and women who served with the six multi-national squadrons which formed the Banff Strike Wing at R.A.F. Banff between September 1944 and May 1945. Under the command of Group Captain the Hon. Max Aitken the mixed Mosquito and Beaufighter units mounted concentrated attacks on German surface vessels and U-boats in the North Sea and along the Norwegian coast. Their success in the closing months of World War II was important in the defeat of Germany and strike wing aircraft operating from the airfield near here inflicted heavy damage on enemy shipping and supply routes. Many thousands of tons of vital iron ore and other supplies were lost to the German forces as a result of rocket and cannon attacks carried out by this gallant strike wing. Losses amongst R.A.F. commonwealth and Norwegian squadrons were high. More than 80 aircrew gave their lives flying with the R.A.F. Banff Strike Wing."

Meteorology – From March 1 1941 all five specialist meteorological units then existing were placed under the operational control of Coastal Command. They were designated as Nos. 1401 to 1405 Flights and each was the responsibility of the Group in whose area it was based. Up until this point it had been felt that the Germans had been putting more resource than the British into weather forecasting and had been getting results to match.

An image captured by an ice patrol over the Denmark Strait.

The original meteorological flight had been formed at Eastchurch, Kent, in 1924 and had spent a considerable part of the inter-war period at Duxford, Cambridgeshire.

As the war progressed more met units were added, partly as a result of the availability of suitable aircraft, including Hudsons. Pressure from Bomber Command, particularly concerned not to send off aircraft if regaining their bases would be difficult, was often a factor in the decisions taken. From the spring of 1943 Bomber Command had its own met flight.

It was a notable feature of the meteorological flights that daily sorties, including vertical ascents, were carried out in virtually any weather conditions.

Metox – A receiving device named after a French firm which produced it under duress. Metox enabled German submarines to detect ASV transmissions from Allied aircraft. The steady introduction of Metox in 1942 was one of the many instances during the U-boat war, when an advance in technology gave one side or the other an advantage.

Mid Ocean Gap – See Atlantic Gap.

Mount Batten – Rocky outcrop on peninsula in Plymouth Sound. A Royal Navy seaplane base was established there in the First World War and was known as Cattewater. This passed to the RAF and was renamed Mount Batten in 1928. Amongst others, the T. E. Lawrence biographer, Michael Korda, attributes the suggestion for the name change to Lawrence, who served there.

A Sunderland was destroyed at the base in a German air attack in November 1940.

Sunderland squadrons based at Mount Batten during the Second World War included No. 10 Squadron, RAAF and No. 461, RAAF, formed at Mount Batten in April 1942 from a nucleus of the Australian No. 10 Squadron. No. 461 later moved to Hamworthy Junction, in Poole Harbour and then to Pembroke Dock.

No. 10 Squadron was the only Australian squadron to serve in the European theatre throughout the war. It had been formed at Point Cook, near Melbourne on July 1 1939, with a mixture of aircraft, but, at the end of that month, personnel from the squadron were sent to Britain to train on Sunderlands. On October 7 the Australian Government announced that the squadron would remain in the UK to contribute to the war effort. It was initially stationed at Pembroke

Dock. The squadron's motto was "Strike First" and it suffered 161 fatal casualties during the war.

For a time in the post-war years Mount Batten was the main base of the RAF Marine Branch.

N

North Coates – "North Cotes" is the traditional local spelling of the village after which this Lincolnshire airfield was named. An RFC field was established late in the First World War, but it closed in the middle of 1919. An armament practice camp operated on the site from 1927. The designation "RAF North Coates" was applied from February 1940, when Coastal Command moved in. Squadrons based at North Coates during the Second World War included, Nos. 235, 236, 248 and 407. The North Coates Strike Wing claimed 150,000 tons of enemy shipping destroyed, but lost more than 240 aircrew.

Post war uses included as a base for Bloodhound surface-to-air missiles. The RAF left the airfield in 1990.

A group photograph of personnel of 'A' Flight, No. 59 Squadron in front of a Lockheed Hudson at North Coates in July 1942. Note the broken wooden wheel mounted on the Hudson's nose, this forming part of the squadron's badge.

Northwood – Eastbury Park, near Northwood, Middlesex was the headquarters of Coastal Command from 1939 to 1969. The transfer of the HQ from Lee–on–Solent represented a move closer to the centre of affairs.

The officers' mess at Northwood was situated in a house built in the 1850s for Lord Palmerston, which was known as the Chateau de Madrid and passed through a number of uses until it was purchased by the RAF in 1938. This building was destroyed by fire in 1969.

Northwood remains in service use as the UK's principal military headquarters site.

There is a Coastal Command commemorative window at Northwood, described thus on www.gov.uk.

"In the centre of the window stands the figure of a typical Coastal Command aircrew – pilots, navigators, signallers, radar operators, flight engineers or gunners all looked much the same although of many nationalities: Polish, Czechoslovakian, Dutch, Norwegian and United States squadrons joined forces in the maritime air battle in close and friendly partnership with the Australian, New Zealand, Canadian, South African and United Kingdom squadrons of Coastal Command.

"They fought together as a band of brothers and had the same determination to seek out and destroy the enemy wherever he was to be found.

"This particular aircrew symbolises their everyday task; he is dressed in his normal flying kit and is flashing his Aldis lamp the recognition signal of the day to the nearest corvette or destroyer guarding the convoy to be joined.

"No signal was so welcome to those who sailed in the convoyed ships and the majority of threatened convoys were met day or night, irrespective of weather, throughout the war.

"The central figure stands upon a pile of the weapons used in the anti-U-boat and anti-enemy shipping war – the depth charge, the torpedo and the bomb being the most prominent.

"Below this are the convoys which were – in conjunction with the ships of the Royal and Allied Navies – the aircrews' daily task to guard and here can be seen the signs of enemy activity and our counter-attacks.

"In this lower part of the window is symbolised the hardest fought victory during which the men at sea and in the air fought with their various craft, the weapons, the fuel and the many scientific devices and instruments designed, fashioned or produced by the thousands of anonymous men and women working behind the scenes in many different countries.

"It also symbolises the work of those who planned and directed the war at sea and co-ordinated the allied effort.

"Above and beyond the central figure are two hands clasping the Royal Navy and Royal Air Force ensigns, typifying the marriage of these two great services for their triple task of finding the enemy, striking the enemy and protecting our ships.

"Behind and framing the ensigns and dominating all the top of the window is the sun at dawn as seen by those thousands of aircrew who flew against the enemy over the vast expanse of sea of some ten million square miles and this will symbolise to many the relief felt by those upon the sea and in the air that another day had started and with God's help our ships were a day nearer safety.

"The badges of the subordinate formations of Coastal Command adorn the sides of the window, while the Command badge is in the place of honour at the top. Those formations without badges are shown at the base of the window below the words Constant Endeavour – the Coastal Command motto: never were such words so well chosen.

"On either side of the motto the Blue and Red Ensigns are included to remind us of the heroic endurance of the Royal Fleet Auxiliary, the Merchant Navy and the fishing fleets. The badges of the Royal Air Force and the Royal Navy flank the main window in the adjacent top side panels, thus completing the picture."

An officer who is often mentioned in connection with his service at Northwood is Captain D. V. Peyton-Ward RN, who was the Senior Naval Staff Officer, but seems to have performed a rather wider role in the battles fought by Coastal Command. Indeed, Marshal of the Royal Air Force Lord Douglas of Kirtleside wrote that, "No account of Coastal Command's activities would be complete without mention of 'P-W', as he was known to everybody. He had served in submarines in the First World War, and in having the mind of a submariner he could sense just what action was likely to be taken by the U-boat commanders against whom we were waging a constant battle."

Peyton-Ward had been invalided out of the Royal Navy, between the wars, as a result of arthritis, but he re-joined and spent all of the Second World War with Coastal Command.

Douglas added that "P-W" was frequently in pain, but did not allow this to affect his work, he seemed to be constantly on duty and was an "outstanding success". Peyton-Ward was made CBE and died in 1976.

Norwegian Campaign – From the earliest days of the war Norway, at first neutral, was a matter of concern to the British Government. In December 1939, for instance, Winston Churchill, then First Lord of the Admiralty, circulated a memorandum in which he propounded the need for drastic measures to prevent iron ore for Germany being shipped from the ports of Norway. Pointing out that German U-boats were already operating in Norwegian waters, he proposed that they be mined, with a view to forcing the ships carrying the ore into international waters where they could be intercepted. At the same time the Foreign Office was discussing German concerns that Russian aggression against Norway and Sweden might lead to the Soviet Union acquiring the supplies of ore.

By January 1940 the British Government had formed the view that if Scandinavian iron ore could be denied to Germany then Hitler would end the war. To this end a blockade of the Norwegian port of Narvik was contemplated, or even an invasion of northern Norway to take the ore deposits by force. It was hoped that Norway and Sweden might be manoeuvred into the war on the British side.

Schemes of this sort continued to be considered, though not put into action, until they were overtaken by events.

On April 9 1940, German forces invaded Norway and Britain and France went to the aid of the Norwegians. Immediately Coastal Command was authorised to attack any ships sailing in the Skagerrak. This was the strait between the southwest coast of Sweden, the southeast coast of Norway and the Jutland Peninsula of Denmark, which links the North Sea with, by extension, the Baltic.

In the campaign, fought over a period of two months, there were many mistakes and some successes on the Allied side, but the German invasion of France and the Low Countries ended any hope that Norway might be saved.

A significant contribution by Coastal Command to the campaign was the reconnaissance sorties flown by Hudsons and Sunderlands.

The two-day debate in the House of Commons on the Norwegian campaign, on May 7/8 1940 was described by Roy Jenkins, parliamentarian and biographer of Churchill as, "by a clear head both the most dramatic and the most far-reaching in its consequences of any parliamentary debate of the 20th century." In concluding his speech, the Labour leader, Clement Attlee declared, "It is not Norway alone. Norway comes as the culmination of many other discontents. People are saying that those mainly responsible for the conduct of affairs are men who have had an almost uninterrupted career of failure. Norway followed Czechoslovakia and Poland. Everywhere the story is 'too late'."

In the following days, Neville Chamberlain left office as Prime Minister and was replaced by Churchill, who later wrote of this juncture in British history:

"Now at last the slowly-gathered, long-pent-up fury of the storm broke upon us. Four or five millions of men met each other in the first shock of the most merciless of all the wars of which record has been kept. Within a week the front in France, behind which we had been accustomed to dwell through the hard years of the former war and the opening phase of this, was to be irretrievably broken."

O

Operational Research Unit – Towards the end of his time as AOC in C, Sir Frederick Bowhill appointed a Scientific Adviser in the form of Professor P. M. S. Blackett. As John Terraine pointed out, this led to the development of the Operational Research Unit, led by Blackett and enjoying the services of five Fellows of the Royal Society, including Blackett, the others being Sir John Kendrew, Professor E. J. Williams, Professor C. H. Waddington and Professor J. M. Robertson.

Scientific matters in relation to all aspects of Coastal Command were scrutinised by the committee, with much attention being given to the fight against the U-boats.

Patrick Maynard Stuart Blackett (1897–1974) had been a cadet at the Royal Naval College, Dartmouth when war broke out in 1914. He was present at both the Battle of the Falkland Islands and the Battle of Jutland, but left the Navy in 1919. He graduated with First Class Honours from Cambridge in 1921, was elected to a fellowship of Magdalene College and was a research student under Ernest Rutherford at the Cavendish Laboratory, the physics department of the University of Cambridge. A fellowship of King's College followed.

In the 1930s Blackett headed a laboratory at Birkbeck College, London, and worked with Metropolitan-Vickers on the development of an electromagnet. He became Langworthy Professor of Physics at the University of Manchester. Blackett was highly interested in military matters and sat on the sub-committee on aerial defence, chaired by Henry Tizard, much concerned with the development of radar.

When war came again Blackett worked at the Royal Aircraft Establishment, Farnborough, on bomb-sight development, then, in August 1940, took his knowledge of radar to Anti-Aircraft Command, where he was scientific adviser to the Commander in Chief, General Sir Frederick Pile Bt. Later in the war, some of Blackett's opinions stirred up controversy; for instance, he argued against saturation bombing and the deliberate targeting of civilian homes.

In peacetime, high academic posts held by Blackett included that of Pro-Vice Chancellor of the University of Manchester. He was appointed CH and OM. In 1964 he declined a Life Peerage, but accepted one in 1969.

P

Pembroke Dock – The Royal Dockyard at Pembroke Dock closed in the mid-1920s and the RAF arrived in 1930. In June of the following year No. 210 Squadron, operating Short Southamptons, was moved to south west Wales from Felixstowe.

In March 1933 Pembroke Dock and No. 210 Squadron received a new CO, in the form of a man who would go on to be one of the major figures of the Second World War. However, the tenure of Wing Commander Arthur Harris was brief. After five months he was promoted to Group Captain and posted to the Air Ministry.

Harris's biographer, Henry Probert, wrote, "Of all his many postings this was the one that Harris enjoyed most. He had long wanted to command a 'boat' squadron. He felt this aspect of aviation was encumbered by an unnecessary mystique based on largely spurious nautical lore, and was keen not only to try his hand at it but to prove that flying boats, just like land-based aircraft, could be operated in the dark." His promotion after so short a period was, therefore, not entirely congenial to him. According to one of the pilots who served under Harris he did demonstrate "Cat's Eyes" ability at night.

At the height of the Battle of the Atlantic almost 100 flying boats, most of them Sunderlands, were based in and around Pembroke Dock.

RAF involvement at "PD" largely came to an end with the withdrawal of the Sunderland from UK service in 1957.

Pembroke Dock Sunderland Trust – The Trust, a registered charity, was established in 2006, with particular support from Chevron Refinery, Pembroke and the Milford Haven Port Authority. In 2009 the Flying Boat Visitor Centre opened.

The Centre tells, in particular, the story of Sunderland Mk I T9044, of No. 210 Squadron, which sank in a gale in November 1940 and remained missing for many years. Eventually it was discovered by divers. It is gradually being recovered, with many parts now conserved and displayed, including the remains of two Bristol Pegasus XXII radials.

A particular part of the Sunderland Trust's work is developing the Pembroke Dock Archive. This is located in the Georgian Fleet Surgeon's House in the former Dockyard. In spring 2013 around sixty volunteers were engaged in copying and conserving the Pembroke Dock Collection – covering not only RAF flying boat history but the local community's connections with the Royal Navy and the Army.

Writing in the May 2013 issue of *Britain at War* magazine, John Evans, project leader for the Trust, described an historic document in the collection:

"During one reunion a heavy bag was left anonymously at the shop. When I first looked into it I realised, instantly, that I had history on my hands.

"This is the unofficial war history of one of PD's most famous RAF units, No. 228 Squadron. It covers the whole war period, September 1939 – June 1945, and although it has many gaps it is a hugely important document.

"Here are contemporary accounts of milestones in 228's wartime story – of the dramatic and headline grabbing rescue of the crew of the *Kensington Court* on 18 September 1939 by two Sunderlands; of the ill-fated Norwegian campaign; excursions into the Mediterranean air war, and a long trans-Africa flight made by two Sunderlands in 1941.

"Here, too, is much day-by-day detail of 228's triumphs and tragedies in the Battle of the Atlantic – from Scotland, Northern Ireland and, finally, PD.

"One of 228's tragic chapters centred on the last flight of Sunderland W4026 which crashed at Dumbeath, Scotland, on August 25 1942 when taking Air Commodore HRH The Duke of Kent to Iceland. The Duke and all but one of those aboard were killed. The war diary has revealing insights into the personal cost to the squadron, which included the loss of its new CO, Wing Commander T. L. Moseley, and experienced Australian skipper Flight Lieutenant Frank Goyen.

"For some years the war diary donor remained a mystery but I now know that he was an airman who 'liberated' the book in June 1945 as the squadron disbanded, its job done."

The stricken *Kensington Court* seen from a Sunderland of No. 228 Squadron during the rescue operation.

The SS *Kensington Court*, of the Court Line, was an early U-boat victim, being shelled without warning and sunk on September 18 1939 by *U-32*. The ship was carrying cereals from Rosario, Argentina, and went down between Fastnet and Bishop Rock. No. 228 Squadron was heavily involved in the rescue of crew members.

In October 1939 *The War Illustrated* recorded that, "The story of the rescue of the officers and crew of the SS *Kensington Court* adds a remarkable page to the history of the RAF. The ship, on her way from Argentina to Birkenhead, was stopped by fire from a U-Boat when nearing the English coast and 34 men were compelled to leave her. An SOS had been sent out before the *Kensington Court* sunk, and soon after the overloaded boat carrying 34 had pushed off, a flying-boat appeared and alighted nearby, followed soon after by a second. Eventually all 34 men were transferred to a collapsible rubber boat launched by one of the 'planes and carried to the aircraft. A few hours later they were safe in England."

Photographic Reconnaissance/Interpretation – By the outbreak of the Second World War specialised photo reconnaissance had almost disappeared from the RAF and was in a far worse state than at the end of the previous world war. Taylor Downing suggests that in September 1939 there were only seven trained photo interpreters in the RAF and there were also a very few specialists in the Army.

It was planned that aerial photography (normally from 10,000 feet) would be carried out by Lysanders (for the Army) and Blenheims (for the RAF). The Lysander was very slow and the Blenheim too was no match for the German fighters, not least when encumbered by photographic equipment. Blenheims flew eighty-nine PR operations in the first four months of the war, of which forty-four did not produce usable photographs and during which sixteen aircraft were lost.

There was an alternative approach and this came from Sidney Cotton, a brilliant, turbulent, confrontational and wealthy Australian, who had served as a pilot in the Royal Naval Air Service in the Great

War. He was also the inventor of the Sidcot flying suit, still in significant use by the RAF in the 1939–1945 war.

Around a year before the German invasion of Poland, Cotton was recruited by the British Secret Intelligence Service and, using Lockheed 12As, and initially in co-operation with the French, began photographing German military installations, while purporting to be making business flights. On one occasion he had to evade a German fighter sent up when suspicions were aroused. Cotton was in Berlin

The *Bismarck* (left of centre) caught by a PR aircraft just before setting sail on her first and last sortie.

as war was about to break out and escaped narrowly. He and his crew member obtained long distance photographs of German naval ships at Wilhelmshaven as they flew back to Britain.

Reconnaissance was also being carried out off the German coast by, for example, Commander (Charles) Herbert Lightoller, then well into his 60s, who, in 1912, had been one of the surviving officers of RMS *Titanic*. "Lights" Lightoller and his wife undertook surveys in their diesel yacht *Sundowner* (later, under Lightoller's command, a Dunkirk "Little Ship", with one of his sons and a sea scout as crew) while maintaining the guise of an elderly couple on holiday.

With the onset of war there was much toing and froing over the best way to make use of Cotton and the most suitable way to fit such a maverick into the war effort. It should also be recorded that another who saw clearly the need for much more attention to be paid to photo reconnaissance was Air Chief Marshal Sir Edgar Ludlow-Hewitt, the often-criticised AOC in C at Bomber Command.

A unit under Cotton was established at Heston airfield, Middlesex. It was outside the normal RAF structure, though there was a reporting line to Fighter Command. In a paper submitted to the Air Ministry, Cotton argued that he should be provided with Spitfires, despite Fighter Command's desperate need for Spitfires for combat. Eventually two were obtained and worked well in their new role not withstanding many doubts being expressed over the viability of fitting a camera and extra fuel tank.

Cotton and the civil servant, Sir Maurice Dean (who presumably was in a position to know), claimed that Air Chief Marshal Dowding at Fighter Command had personally agreed to the Spitfires being allocated to PR. Elsewhere this is disputed.

Controversy over Cotton's activities continued, but this was somewhat mitigated and quality of results improved by using the Aircraft Operating Company, an aerial survey business. More Spitfires were also obtained.

Cotton operated from France during the Blitzkrieg, but was removed from his post on his return and played little further part in the war.

Bomber Command argued that it should take responsibility for PR, while the Royal Navy stressed the vital need for information on what the German navy was doing. In the event the Photographic Reconnaissance Unit, as it was now to be called, was placed in Coastal Command, with Wing Commander Geoffrey Tuttle, who had previously worked with Cotton, as the man in charge.

Expansion was now rapid. 'A' Flight of the PRU was located at Wick in the north of Scotland, while 'B' Flight went to St Eval, Cornwall and 'C' and 'D' Flights were at Heston.

The Aircraft Operating Company at Wembley became the Photographic Interpretation Unit. The PIU was commanded by Squadron Leader Peter Riddell who moved over from Bomber Command.

Control of photo reconnaissance and interpretation was placed under Coastal Command, despite the bomber leadership wishing to retain its own facilities. When bomb damage at Heston and Wembley became an issue, the PR aircraft were moved to Benson in Oxfordshire and, after some fits and starts, interpretation was centralised at the eighteenth century Danesfield House near Marlow, Buckinghamshire, with an inspiring view over the River Thames. The new operation incorporated Naval and Army interpretation, the modelling work formerly undertaken at the Royal Aircraft Establishment, Farnborough and damage assessment from Bomber Command. Benson, though safer than Heston, proved not to be immune from Luftwaffe attacks.

An RAF Directorate of Intelligence was established and took control of these operations. Photo reconnaissance continued to be an operational responsibility of Coastal Command.

Among the many subsequent achievements for PRU aircraft was, on February 11 1942, the filming of large German warships at Brest clearly preparing to put to sea. The benefit of this information was not as great as it should have been, as explained in the "Channel Dash" entry in this Dictionary.

A German cruiser in dock at Brest. A Coastal Command aircraft took this photograph from 500 ft.

Danesfield House had to be incorporated in the RAF hierarchy and, with the service's habit of using the names of nearby villages, the name that has gone down in the history of the Second World War is RAF Medmenham. Danesfield was purchased after the war by the Air Ministry and remained in the hands of the RAF until 1977. Today it is a hotel and spa.

As the PRU grew and grew, flights were formed into squadrons.

In his book, *Spies in the Sky*, Taylor Downing recorded that Air Chief Marshal Bowhill regarded the three crucial qualifications for pilots being recruited to reconnaissance work as considerable experience, outstanding ability to navigate and "above average classification as a pilot for common sense". Bowhill apparently regarded former bomber and army co-operation flyers as far more suited to the reconnaissance role than fighter men.

R

Ranks – RAF and Luftwaffe ranks were not precisely equivalent. Some examples of approximate equivalents are:-

Corporal = Gefreiter
Sergeant = Unteroffizier, Unterfeldwebel
Flight Sergeant = Feldwebel
Warrant Officer = Stabsfeldwebel, Oberfeldwebel
Pilot Officer = Leutnant
Flying Officer = Oberleutnant
Flight Lieutenant = Hauptmann
Squadron Leader = Major
Wing Commander = Oberstleutnant
Group Captain = Oberst

A Sergeant Air Gunner in position in a Coastal Command Catalina.

The RAF rank structure as it is known today was introduced on August 27 1919. From April 1 1918, when the RAF was formed, until the new designations came into force, Army ranks had been used. As the new service was an amalgam of the Royal Naval Air Service and the Royal Flying Corps (a part of the Army), the 1919 ranks represented a combination of the practices of the two services. The RAF abolished the rank of Sergeant Major in 1933 and Warrant Officer Class 2 during the Second World War.

Roadstead – A low-level attack against shipping in coastal waters.

Rover – Armed reconnaissance by a small number of aircraft acting independently and given a specific area to search for enemy shipping.

The climax of a Rover. This photograph was taken on August 12 1944 from the No. 248 Squadron Mosquito of Squadron Leader "Tubby" Randall, DFC. The German armed trawler under attack was one of a number of enemy ships located in the Gironde Estuary.

Royal Air Force Volunteer Reserve (RAFVR) – An organisation founded in 1936 with the prime purpose of providing a pool of additional aircrew for use in the event of war. There were to be no distinctions of class and major cities were regarded as fertile recruiting grounds.

In a document prepared by the Air Council to "sell" the idea to the Treasury, this point was stressed when it was explained that the new organisation would welcome, "the whole middle class in the widest sense of that term, namely the complete range of the output of the public and secondary schools". Later it remarked that, "it would be inappropriate to grade the members on entry as officers or airmen according to their social class; entry will accordingly be on a common footing, as airman pilot or observer and promotions to commissioned rank will be made at a later stage in accordance with the abilities of leadership actually displayed."

At the start of the Second World War the strength of the RAFVR stood at well over 6,000 pilots and well over 1,000 observers, as well as almost 2,000 Wireless Operators/Air Gunners. From that point the RAFVR became the principal route of entry for aircrew into the RAF. One advantage of this arrangement, appealing to bureaucratic minds, was the reduction in the potential need to pay pensions, which it involved.

A major part in the conception of the RAFVR was played by Air Commodore (later Marshal of the Royal Air Force) Arthur Tedder, then the RAF's Director of Training, though the "Citizen Air Force" that he advocated was not what transpired.

Today, in much changed form, the VR continues to support the RAF in a variety of ways.

Royal Auxiliary Air Force – See Auxiliary Air Force.

Runnymede Memorial – Inevitably, many of the personnel lost while serving with Coastal Command in the Second World War have no known grave. There were those who were lost over the sea and were never found. In addition, the Royal Navy often buried at sea bodies that its ships discovered.

People serving in the RAF without a known grave are remembered on various memorials around the world, depending on the geographical area from which they went missing. The Runnymede Memorial, on Cooper's Hill, overlooking the Thames at Englefield Green between Windsor and Egham, contains the names of over 20,000 personnel who were lost flying from airfields in the United Kingdom and northern and western Europe.

The memorial was designed by Edward (later Sir Edward) Maufe with sculpture by Vernon Hill. It was opened by Her Majesty the Queen on October 17 1953 and can be visited every day apart from Christmas Day and New Year's Day.

Edward Maufe had been born in 1882 with the surname Muff, but changed the name by deed poll in his twenties. He served as an officer in the Royal Artillery in the First World War. As an architect with his own practice, Maufe was influenced by the Arts and Crafts Movement. His work included Kelling Hall in Norfolk, the Palace of Industry at the Wembley exhibition of 1924, Guildford Cathedral, and the rebuilding of the Middle Temple and Gray's Inn in London, following Second World War bomb damage.

Between 1943 and 1969 Maufe was first Principal Architect UK and then Chief Architect and Artistic Adviser to the Imperial War Graves Commission (renamed Commonwealth War Graves Commission in 1960) which administers the Runnymede Memorial. His services to the IWGC brought Maufe a knighthood in 1954. He died in 1974.

The Imperial War Graves Commission was established in 1917 and, across the world, it cared for the graves of UK and Commonwealth military personnel lost in the two world wars. Its founder was Fabian (later Sir Fabian) Ware (1869–1949), one-time editor of the *Morning Post* newspaper. Its funding comes mainly from the governments of the United Kingdom, Canada, Australia, New Zealand, South Africa and India.

S

St Eval – With war looming and as part of the RAF expansion plan, a need was identified for an airfield in the southwest of England which would provide a base for anti-shipping and anti-submarine activities. The result was a decision to build at St Eval on the north Cornish coast, near Newquay. The acquisition of the land was controversial, as the work involved the demolition of St Eval village, apart from the church, other homes and ancient tumuli. Parts of two farms were acquired. The airfield opened shortly after the outbreak of war.

Fighter aircraft were based at St Eval for a time and it therefore played its part in the Battle of Britain. Coastal Command squadrons at St Eval in 1940 included No. 217 Squadron (Ansons and Beauforts) and No. 236 Squadron (Blenheims). The Luftwaffe attacked St Eval on a number of occasions, causing damage and casualties. A disaster occurred in 1943 when a Liberator and a Whitley collided.

As the war progressed, Liberators equipped with Leigh Lights became a major feature of St Eval. RAF St Eval closed in 1959, though casual use by nearby RAF St Mawgon continued for a time.

The church at St Eval remains a local landmark. It is dedicated to St Uvelus, stands 300 feet above sea level, dates back to the thirteenth century and was constructed on the site of a Celtic shrine. The present tower, sixty feet tall, was built in 1727 and the pulpit dates from 1638.

"It seemed most appropriate that the CCMAA decided at their 2004 AGM that the Association needed a spiritual home and concluded that St Eval was the obvious choice. The church has provided a physical landmark for mariners and latterly airmen for centuries; it is the final resting place for many of our comrades; the community of St Eval made great sacrifices when the airfield was built, to provide an operating base for Coastal Command units and to this day the church has continued to give spiritual inspiration and comfort to serving RAF personnel.

"Our Chairman, Andrew Neal, consequently wrote to the Vicar, the Rev Graham Shield, and the PCC asking that the CCMAA be allowed to 'adopt' St Eval as 'The Church for the Coastal Command and Maritime Air Association'. After discussions and consultations with the Diocese, this was approved." (From the CCMAA website).

Saro (Saunders Roe) A.36 Lerwick – A flying boat now rarely remembered, it was intended to replace a number of earlier designs and to serve alongside the Short Sunderland in roles such as reconnaissance, anti-submarine and convoy protection. It proved to be a failure and served operationally in very limited numbers, with aircraft being lost to accidents, sometimes when wing floats broke off. Some Lerwicks went to the RCAF. Nos. 240 and 209 Squadrons were briefly RAF operators of the aircraft, the latter going over to Catalinas in April 1941.

The Lerwick first flew in November 1938. It was a two-engine high wing monoplane.

Saro (Saunders Roe) A.27 London – A reconnaissance flying boat which served with the RAF between 1936 and 1941. Up to 2,000 lb of bombs could be carried. The RCAF was also an operator.

Scarecrow – A term from the Great War, relating to aircraft disrupting the work of U-boats by causing them to dive hastily. With the aircraft initially available to Coastal Command this was sometimes the best outcome that could be hoped for in the early part of the campaign against the submarine menace.

Ships (assistance to) – Many ships, Royal Navy, Merchant Navy and neutral, were assisted by Coastal Command. An especially remembered occasion when the Command came to help a Royal Navy vessel in distress, was the case of the K-class destroyer and flotilla leader, HMS *Kelly*. In May 1940, during the Norwegian campaign, *Kelly* was torpedoed by a German E-boat and badly damaged. She was taken in tow by the tug *Great Emperor* and eventually returned to British waters despite attacks by E-boats and aircraft. Coastal Command Hudsons fought the enemy aircraft in the vicinity of *Kelly* and thwarted an attempt to intervene by at least one submarine.

Kelly was the ship from which Captain Lord Louis Mounbatten commanded the Fifth Destroyer Flotilla. He would later be Chief

The badly damaged HMS *Kelly* photographed by a Hudson of Coastal Command's No. 224 Squadron on May 10 1940, while the aircraft was acting as escort during the destroyer's journey to port after it was torpedoed off Norway.

of Combined Operations, Supreme Commander South East Asia, Viceroy of India, First Sea Lord and Chief of Defence Staff and was created Viscount Mountbatten of Burma in 1946. The ship was sunk off Crete in 1941.

"You will be glad to hear that HMS *Kelly* has succeeded in arriving safely at the Tyne. I should like to thank you for your co-operation in this operation. Your aircraft must have had a difficult job, but the successful conclusion of the operation in which they played their part so well will, I am sure, make them feel it was all worthwhile." Signal sent by the Commander in Chief Rosyth to Coastal Command.

The sinking of a civilian ship which was utilised by the British for propaganda purposes, was the loss of the SS *Arandora Star* on July 2 1940. The ship was torpedoed by *U-47* while northwest of Ireland, sailing alone from Liverpool to St John's. Newfoundland. She was carrying well over 1,000 Germans and Italians – internees and prisoners of war. Many lives were lost.

The Air Ministry publication, *Coastal Command*, covering the years 1939–1942, recorded that a Sunderland was tasked to find survivors. It discovered thirteen lifeboats and others who had escaped from the vessel clinging to wreckage. After dropping, food, first aid supplies and "Mae West" lifejackets, the aircraft located the Royal Canadian Navy destroyer *St Laurent* and spent several hours guiding the warship to the scene and assisting it to find survivors.

Short S.25 Sunderland – The Short Sunderland is an aircraft which, more than most, conjures up images of Coastal Command. This is helped, of course, by the fact that it was one of the few major types developed specifically with maritime operations in mind.

In addition, and ensuring still more attention, the Sunderland was in the same family as the Empire class flying boats, which Imperial Airways and then BOAC used to connect the UK with Dominions and colonies.

As was the frequent practice with British military flying boats, the Sunderland was given the name of a maritime location. The type made its first flight, in October 1937, taking off from the River Medway at Rochester, Kent, where Short Brothers was building Sunderlands. Later, some aircraft were produced in Belfast and by Blackburn Aircraft at Dumbarton. Reconnaissance was the original purpose of the Sunderland, but, in Coastal Command service, it fulfilled a wide range of roles.

The Sunderland I had four Bristol Pegasus XXll engines. First deliveries to a squadron arrived at Seletar, Singapore, for No. 230 Squadron in the middle of 1938. This was a time when RAF flying boat squadrons were operating a mixed bag of often elderly aircraft. No. 230 Squadron, having been disbanded in 1923, had been reformed at Pembroke Dock, eleven years later with Singapores.

When the Second World War came, the type's ability to defend itself would cause it to be named the "Flying Porcupine" by the Luftwaffe. A considerable number of other entries in this book make reference to the outstanding service of the Sunderland with Coastal Command in

Short Sunderland W6077 'U' of No. 461 Squadron.

wartime. Having taken part in the Berlin airlift, the Sunderland finally left RAF service in 1959.

What is a Flying Boat? – explained by the website of the Pembroke Dock Sunderland Trust:

"A flying boat is an aircraft which, instead of using a wheeled undercarriage to take off and land from the land, does so from a water 'runway'.

"Flying boats have boat hulls and keels with floats underneath each wing to give them stability. Before the advent of large transport aircraft, flying boats were the only aircraft capable of flying long distances with a sizeable cargo or passenger load. Flying boats helped open up far-flung parts of the British Empire to air travel in the 1930s."

Sinclair, Sir Archibald Bt (1890–1970) – A leader of Liberal MPs who was Secretary of State for Air 1940–1945. He had served in the Life Guards and, on the Western Front, as second in command to Winston Churchill in the 6th battalion, Royal Scots Fusiliers. He was a close friend of Churchill and often, during the war, thought of as under the Prime Minister's thumb. He was frequently at odds with Lord Beaverbrook in Beaverbrook's term as Minister of Aircraft Production. Sinclair was created Viscount Thurso in 1952.

"Within the Cabinet," according to J. T. Moore-Brabazon, "the bullying, especially of Archibald Sinclair, was tremendous." Others remembered Churchill treating him with "half-serious levity … he used to bully … poor old Archie … [and] jump down his throat every time he opened his mouth." (Gerard J. de Groot in *The Life of Sir Archibald Sinclair*. Moore-Brabazon, later Lord Brabazon of Tara, was Minister of Transport 1940–1941 and Minister of Aircraft Production 1941–1942).

Sir John Colville, Prime Ministerial Private Secretary, took the view that Churchill admired Sinclair for his personal qualities, rather than his ministerial competence. In later life Colville revised his opinion that Sinclair had been bullied by Churchill.

Sir Archibald Sinclair pictured during the Second World War.

Slatter, Air Marshal Sir Leonard (1894–1961) – Born in South Africa, Slatter came to Britain aged ten. He joined the Royal Navy in 1914 and the Royal Naval Air Service in the following year. He served with various units in the UK and on the continent and was credited with destroying seven enemy aircraft. In the RAF from 1918, Slatter saw action in Russia, served in Turkey and Malta and commanded the RAF High Speed Flight. He commanded a number of fighter squadrons and various RAF stations including Hornchurch and Tangmere.

At the outbreak of the Second World War, Slatter was Senior Air Staff Officer at No. 1 Group in Bomber Command before going to Iraq. Command of various Groups culminated in his appointment to lead No. 15 Group, Coastal Command in 1943. He was Air Officer, Commanding in Chief, Coastal Command, June 1945 until 1948.

Slatter was awarded the DSC and bar and DFC and was made KBE and CB.

Slessor, Marshal of the Royal Air Force Sir John (1897–1979) – "Jack" Slessor, who was educated at Haileybury College, suffered from polio as a child. This led to his initial rejection for service in the Army. However, he made use of a family connection to enter the Royal Flying Corps.

Slessor learned to fly at Brooklands and had a brief spell with No. 23 Squadron at Suttons Farm (later RAF Hornchurch), before joining No. 17 Squadron and serving in Sinai and the Sudan. He was wounded and awarded the MC. On recovery, he was a Flight Commander in France with No. 5 Squadron and commanded the Central Flying School.

After the First World War, Slessor left the RAF briefly, but returned and took part in the first Hendon Air Display. He went to No. 20 Squadron on the North West Frontier, served at the Air Ministry and attended the RAF Staff College.

In 1925 Squadron Leader Slessor took command of No. 4 Squadron at Farnborough, flying the Bristol F2b in the Army Co–operation role. A close association with the future Lord Trenchard (at the time Chief of the Air Staff) began when Slessor was posted to the Directorate of Operations and Intelligence. He spent four years in the early 1930s as the RAF member of the directing staff.

"Although he viewed this period as a somewhat unreal existence, it provided many friendships which would later be invaluable and enabled him to develop a reputation in service circles for clear thinking and writing, exemplified in his influential book *Air Power and Armies*, published in 1936," (Henry Probert in *High Commanders of the Royal Air Force*).

As a Wing Commander, Slessor led No. 3 (Indian) Wing and narrowly escaped death in the Quetta earthquake. For his leadership of the Wing in the Waziristan operations in what is now Pakistan, he was awarded the DSO.

In the interwar period, Slessor was one of a group of up and coming RAF officers, who have sometimes been described as "disciples" of

Lord Trenchard, the man who shaped the RAF in its early days and continued to exert great influence long after he had ceased to hold office in the service. Others who can be included in this group and who went on to hold wartime posts at or near the top of the service were the Hon Ralph Cochrane, Arthur Harris and "Peter" Portal.

During the years 1937 to 1940 Slessor was at the centre of affairs as Director of Plans at the Air Ministry, before going to Washington DC, with the acquisition of American aircraft for the RAF as a key part of his brief.

From the spring of 1941 Slessor commanded No. 5 Group in Bomber Command, initially with Hampdens, but with the Manchester and then the Lancaster soon arriving. He went back to the Air Ministry as Assistant Chief of Air Staff (Policy).

It was in February 1943 that Slessor took over as Air Officer Commanding in Chief, Coastal Command. He moved the next year to become Air Commander in Chief, Mediterranean and Middle East, with much time occupied with the Italian campaign.

A return to a home post occurred in March 1945 when he took up the role of Air Member for Personnel, with the job of overseeing the release of many men and women and the establishment of an RAF structure suited to the demands of relative peace time.

After a spell as Commandant of the Imperial Defence College, Sir John Slessor was appointed Chief of the Air Staff from January 1 1950, a post he would hold until the last day of 1952. Elevation to Marshal of the Royal Air Force came on June 8 1950.

Dominant matters during Slessor's time as CAS were the Korean War and the need to develop defences against the threat posed by the Soviet Union. Slessor continued to involve himself after stepping down as CAS, writing and broadcasting and often promoting the case for a powerful air force.

"Certainly Slessor deserves recognition as one of the great thinkers about air strategy, and he also proved himself to be one of the RAF's most able operational commanders. Above all, however, he had the staff skills and the ability to get on with leaders at the highest level which proved their worth both in wartime and in dealing with the special challenges that faced him as Chief of the Air Staff." (Air Commodore Henry Probert in *High Commanders of the Royal Air Force*).

Sonobuoy – A device, codenamed "High Tea", used to detect submarines underwater, which was Coastal Command's equivalent to the Asdic used by the Navy. From 1942 they were often dropped from Sunderlands. Details of the weapon were kept highly secret and the enemy's initial reaction was that their purpose was to prevent U-boats travelling on the surface.

Asdic had been developed by the Navy at the end of the First World War and through the interwar years. It sent a sound wave through water, which was reflected if the wave struck a submerged object. Range was established by the length of time taken by the beam to arrive back with the operator. Asdic was called Sonar by the Americans and this word was adapted in "Sonobuoy", which was dropped from the aircraft, floated on the surface of the sea, and transmitted information to operators above.

Squadron – A word inherited by the RAF from both its predecessors, the Royal Naval Air Service and the Royal Flying Corps. A term that denotes a range of units, often equipped with aircraft, but also used by, for example, the RAF Regiment.

As Wing Commander C. G. Jefford wrote in *RAF Squadrons*, "What distinguishes most flying squadrons, however, is that they have a notionally discrete status. Their existence is not conditional upon that of a parent station or wing organisation. A squadron's notional independence is signified by its individual number. This is allocated to it from a centrally controlled series administered at ministry level."

Under attack from aircraft of the Banff Strike Wing, a tanker blows up shortly after leaving the Norwegian port of Kristiansand bound for Arendal on October 15 1944. Bristol Beaufighters of No. 404 Squadron, RCAF are seen over the vessel. One, flown by Warrant Officer Jackson, was hit by debris, but returned to base. The ship had been the Norwegian-owned *Inger Johanne*.

Ian Coleman has contributed the short study below of a particularly distinguished squadron in wartime Coastal Command. In July 1946 the Air Council approved a list of squadron number-plates to be given priority in the RAF's reduced post war circumstances. Longevity and participation in the Battle of Britain were among the criteria used for inclusion in the list, which had been drafted by the Air Historical Branch. However, some squadrons were included whose claim would have failed if the criteria were strictly applied. One example of such a squadron was No. 617, considered to have an especially outstanding wartime record, including the attack on the German dams.

Also included were Nos. 120, 297 and 511 Squadrons. According to Jefford, "These were selected for preservation on the grounds that they were, respectively, the first Very Long Range General Reconnaissance Squadron (and not, as is sometimes stated, because it had sunk the greatest number of U-boats – although this was the case), the first Airborne Forces Squadron and the first Long Range Transport Squadron. A similar case had been submitted in support of No. 172 Squadron, as the first Leigh Light Squadron, but this had failed to find favour."

No. 120 Squadron

Initially, the RAF had no very long range land-based patrol aircraft, but acquired some B-24 Liberators from a French order not delivered before the fall of France. No. 120 Squadron was reformed on 2 June 1941 at Nutts Corner, Belfast, as part of No. 15 Group, Coastal Command, to operate the new Liberator I. Much American equipment was replaced and ASV radar, a four 20mm cannon belly pack and racking for eight depth charges in the bomb bay fitted. After training on unmodified aircraft, 120 began operations on 20 September when Flight Lieutenant Harrison and Flight Lieutenant Bulloch flew anti-submarine patrols. The first B-24 combat action was on 4 October when Flying Officer Llewellyn attacked an FW 200 Condor with cannon west of Ireland, causing damage. On the 23rd, Bulloch made the first U-boat attack, causing slight damage. Bulloch was critical of the official tactic of attacking across the target track with well-spaced depth charges, as he felt it was difficult to inflict fatal damage. He developed the tactic of running up within thirty degrees to the target's track and dropping the weapons closer together, with dramatic results later in his career.

Strikes into the Bay of Biscay and shipping reconnaissance off the Norwegian coast were carried out. During one shipping attack, Bulloch's aircraft was hit by return fire and the rear gunner, Sergeant Hollies, was wounded, being the squadron's first casualty in action. Shortly after, the first fatalities occurred when a Lib crashed into high ground killing five.

On 11 January 1942, Flying Officer Cundy found a U-boat and tanker together and attacked and badly damaged two He 115 float-planes. There were several fatal crashes in the bad winter weather, the next U-boat attack being in May.

The squadron's first loss to enemy action was on 28 May when Flying Officer Walton, returning from convoy escort off the Lofotens, was attacked by three Bf 109s. One was claimed destroyed but, with two engines out, the Lib ditched. Five of the crew drifted to an island in dinghies, though the navigator died. They were captured, but escaped, stole a boat and made for mainland Norway. A month later they reached Sweden. The two pilots received the MC, the engineer the MM and the air gunner the DFM.

In July the squadron moved to Ballykelly. On 16 August the now Squadron Leader Bulloch damaged *U-89*. Two days later he badly damaged *U-653*. To extend coverage a detachment was sent to Reykjavik in Iceland. The squadron's first kill was on 12 October, when a radar contact proved to be *U-597*, which Bulloch sank using his attack tactic.

During October, two Liberators were detached to Egypt for VLR patrols over the central and eastern Mediterranean, to help restrict enemy operations, returning in February 1943.

No. 120's next action came on 5 November around convoy SC107, when Bulloch was directed down an HF/DF bearing to *U-89*, seriously damaging it this time. He later attacked two other contacts. In December convoy HX217 sailed from Halifax, Nova Scotia to the UK but faced a twenty-two-boat wolf pack. On 8 December Bulloch was tasked in support from Iceland and straddled *U-254*, which was unable to dive after a collision with *U-221*. It was sunk. Three hours later the crew attacked two more U-boats. Then, with no depth charges remaining, Bulloch forced down eight U-boats with cannon fire, the result being that the shaken wolf pack lost contact with the convoy. Bulloch was awarded the DSO and four members of the crew were decorated.

During the winter of 1942–1943 the Germans made an increased effort. In February the squadron damaged two U-boats and moved to Aldergrove, with a detachment remaining in Iceland. From there, on the 15th, Flying Officer Turner sank *U-225*. Six days later Squadron Leader Isted, flying from Aldergrove, attacked two U-boats shadowing a convoy. He was probably responsible for the demise of *U-623*.

The Battle of the Atlantic reached a climax in the spring of 1943. On 6 April, Flying Officer Hatherley, operating from Iceland, was credited with the destruction of *U-635*. Next Flying Officer Moffatt damaged *U-594*, forcing it to return to base. The next week the HQ and 'A' Flight moved to Reykjavik, while 'B' Flight used Meek's Field (now Keflavik). A detachment was left at Aldergrove, with many sorties starting at one base and landing at the other. The Germans fielded over sixty U-boats in late April and early May against the convoys. On 23 April Moffatt spotted two submarines and attacked, sinking *U-189*.

On 19 May, Flight Sergeant Stoves attacked a submarine, using three depth charges and two of the new and highly secret acoustic torpedoes. This was believed to be the end of *U-954*, whose crew included the son of Admiral Donitz, though it was also claimed by the convoy escorts. Later in the patrol he forced down several other boats. Next day

Squadron Leader Proctor sank *U-258* and Flight Lieutenant McEwan attacked several others. On 28 May, Flying Officer Fleming-William sank *U-304*. On the 21st Donitz recalled the U-boats, forty-one having been lost in May. On the 15th, Squadron Leader Esler damaged *U-449*, and on the 28th Flight Lieutenant Frazer sank *U-200*, on her way to the Indian Ocean, despite heavy flak which damaged the aircraft. He was awarded a bar to his DFC.

The struggle was renewed in September. Flying from Reykjavik on 20 September, Flight Lieutenant Moffatt attacked a surfaced U-boat with depth charges and cannon, following up with an acoustic torpedo which destroyed *U-338*. Now sonobuoys and better radar were available but the U-boats were staying surfaced to fight it out with enhanced anti-aircraft armament. The Commanding Officer, Wing Commander Longmore and crews were lost, shot down on 4 October by *U-539*. Flight Lieutenant McEwan, escorting the same convoy, sank *U-389*, whilst on a seventeen-hour sortie on 8 October, Warrant Officer Turnbull damaged another. During the next ten days, 120 shared in the destruction of *U-643*, *U-470* and *U-540*, with Liberators from Nos. 59 and 86 Squadrons. In eight months 120 had sunk ten U-boats and shared three more.

With new Mk V Liberators in service, No. 120 Squadron's first contact of 1944 was on 6 March when Flight Lieutenant Kerrigan found a surfaced U-boat and attacked despite heavy flak, severely damaging *U-737*. The aircraft was hard hit with both navigators injured. The first navigator, Flying Officer Rackham, was awarded a DFC for navigating the aircraft to Skitten on two engines. Kerrigan received a DSO.

The squadron moved to Ballykelly, mostly flying patrols off Norway, with a rate of over eighty patrols a month. In support of D-Day the squadron mounted "Cork" patrols (see D-Day entry) in the South West approaches to prevent attacks on the invasion fleets. On 9 June Flight Lieutenant Sherwood sank *U-740* some 200 miles off Lands End, but this was the only success in 1944. There were fewer U-boats now and the new "schnorkel" mast enabled them to recharge batteries submerged.

In December the squadron began re-equipping with the Liberator GR VIII, first seeing action on 22 March 1945 when Squadron Leader White went for a U-boat sighted by a Wellington. Sonobuoys were laid and located the submarine. Two acoustic torpedoes were launched. An explosion was heard after thirteen minutes. White's aircraft was credited with sinking the *U-296*, though the Germans believed it had succumbed to a mine. As the war was ending, on 29 April off Malin Head, Flying Officer Olive attacked a "schnorkel" with depth charges and heard *U-1017* breaking up on sonobuoys. It was 120's final kill. With the rundown of Coastal Command after the German surrender, the squadron was disbanded on 4 June 1945. It was revived at Leuchars on 1 October 1946 when No. 160 Squadron was renumbered.

No. 120 Squadron's record was noteworthy. Its members had been awarded three DSOs and one bar, two MCs, twenty-seven DFCs and two bars, one MM and nine DFMs. The squadron's aircraft are believed to have sunk, or shared in the sinking, of nineteen U-boats and damaged a further ten to be Coastal Command's top scoring squadron.

Strike Wings – From late 1942 "Strike Wings" were formed in Coastal Command with a view to improving the success of attacks on shipping, in particular the convoys bringing supplies of iron ore from the Scandinavian countries along the coast of Europe. The weapons of the Strike Wings were the Beaufighter, starting with the Mk VIC variant and the Mosquito.

For the aircrew, the work was demanding and highly dangerous. It was also a success – records suggest that more than 300 enemy ships were sunk or damaged in attacks carried out by the Strike Wings.

Principal Strike Wing locations were: Banff, Dallachy (near Elgin), Davidstow Moor (Cornwall), Langham (Norfolk), Leuchars, North Coates, Portreath (Cornwall), Strubby (Lincolnshire) and Wick.

"I shall never forget those long grinds over the cold, angry North Sea, flying just above the surface in company with 100 more aircraft. Looking at one's watch and realising with absolute certainty that at the estimated time of arrival on the target plus five minutes, one would either be flying home with a light heart, a prisoner – or dead. It is strange that life could be whittled down to only three alternatives, one of which has got to happen within a short space of time." (Group Captain the Hon Sir Max Aitken Bt, who commanded the Banff Strike Wing, quoted by his daughter, Laura Levi, in *1940* magazine, 2012).

A dedication in *The Strike Wings* by Roy Conyers Nesbit reads as follows:-

In memory of the nine squadrons of the Strike Wings, Coastal Command 143, 144, 235, 236, 248, 254, 404 (RCAF), 455 (RAAF), 489 (RNZAF) with their outriders in 333 (Norwegian) Squadron.

The Mosquitos of No. 333 Squadron specialised in reconnaissance and in attacks on enemy targets in Norway. The squadron also operated Catalinas. Its bases included Banff and a detachment at Sullum Voe (Shetland).

The squadrons of the Strike Wings, "fought in some of the bitterest and bloodiest attacks of the war, all at low level and at close quarters … they suffered heavy casualties in the same proportion as Bomber Command, but they inflicted far greater damage on the enemy in relation to their losses." (Air Chief Marshal Sir Neil Wheeler in his foreword to *The Strike Wings* by Roy Conyers Nesbitt).

"The coastal Strike Wings by contrast flew very low, usually below 500 ft, climbing only slightly to make the actual attack. The flak was nearly always very heavy and so were the casualties; but, if you were hit, you usually went straight into the sea and can have known very little about it, for at most a second or two. I came to the conclusion that death itself was less frightening than pain, certainly in my own case." (Air Chief Marshal Sir Christopher Foxley-Norris, writing in *A Lighter Shade of Blue*).

He had explained that being wounded, crippled, disfigured and, especially, burned, was the greatest fear of many fighter pilots, of which he had been one. In a fighter, in contrast to a strike aircraft, one might be trapped in a burning aircraft falling from 30,000 feet. The knowledge of the likelihood of quick death attacking ships, rather than lingering death or terrible injury, helped him to keep his fears under control.

"What a sight it was! The whole convoy, which a moment before had been sailing peacefully down the coast was now covered by a pall of smoke. Ships were on fire and sinking. Everywhere, dozens of aircraft were diving, firing and turning in all directions. As I broke away, I saw the largest vessel in the convoy with a mass of flames from stem to stern. Just in front of it there came a terrific explosion and steam and water spouted up to 300 or 400 feet. When it subsided, the ship that had been there was there no longer. She blew up without leaving a single trace." (Squadron Leader Jack Davenport, RAAF, describes an attack on a German convoy, just off the coast of southern Norway on July 15 1944. Quoted in *Jack Davenport, Beaufighter Leader* by Kristen Alexander).

The sortie involved forty-four Beaufighters of Nos. 144, 404, 455 and 489 Squadrons. The convoy consisted of four merchant vessels and five escort ships.

Supermarine Sea Otter – A claim to fame of the Sea Otter amphibian was that it was the last biplane to enter RAF service. A step forward from the Walrus, the Sea Otter had an all metal hull and (powered by the Bristol Mercury engine) the ability to lift heavier loads off water and fly longer distances than its forerunner. The first flight was in August 1938 and the first air sea rescue examples to reach Coastal Command arrived in late 1943. A major factor in this long gap was the inevitable preoccupation of Supermarine with developing the Spitfire.

Sea Otters also served in the Far East and with the Fleet Air Arm.

Supermarine Spitfire – It was Supermarine's Chief Designer, R. J. Mitchell, who was responsible for creating the Spitfire and the aircraft was flown for the first time from Eastleigh aerodrome (now Southampton Airport) by Captain Joe "Mutt" Summers on March 5 1936. After Mitchell's death in 1937, Joe Smith played a leading part in the development of the aircraft and its entry into service. He eventually became Supermarine Chief Designer.

The name Spitfire was suggested by a director of Vickers-Armstrong (the Supermarine parent company), Sir Robert Maclean, who used the Elizabethan expression, "a little Spitfire", to describe his daughter Ann, who, as Annie Penrose, died, aged 100, in 2011. The name Spitfire had also been applied unofficially to a previous Mitchell design.

It is claimed that Mitchell commented, that it was, "just the sort of bloody silly name that they would choose". However, if the Air Ministry had had its way, the aircraft might have become the Supermarine Shrew.

The Spitfire entered RAF service with No. 19 Squadron in 1938 and served, in a variety of roles and with major improvements throughout the war. The last operational Spitfire sortie was flown by No. 81 Squadron in Malaya in 1954.

Spitfires in Coastal Command service made many PR and meteorological flights.

Supermarine Stranraer – This was a coastal reconnaissance flying boat, which in the earliest days of its existence was known as the Southampton V, continuing the name of a previous design. Stranraers disappeared from operational RAF service early in the war. They were also flown by the RCAF.

Supermarine Walrus – The design of the Walrus was led by R. J. Mitchell. It was originally the Seagull V, though it was a considerably different aircraft to the previous Seagull. The first flight of a Seagull V took place in 1933. The Walrus was carried by Royal Navy ships, often used for reconnaissance and communications flights. It was also capable of offensive action, carrying bombs or depth charges.

From 1941 when RAF specialist air sea rescue squadrons were established in Coastal Command, the Walrus equipped a number of them.

The Mk II Walrus had a Bristol Pegasus engine, a maximum speed of 135 mph and a service ceiling of 18,500 ft, with a range of 600 miles.

In everyday service parlance, the Walrus was the "Shagbat" or "Steam Chicken".

At least one Walrus pilot was recommended for the VC. The story of the deed of Flight Lieutenant (as he became) Tom Fletcher, who died in 2010, was told in his obituary in the *Daily Telegraph*. At the time Fletcher was a Sergeant with No. 277 Squadron:

"On October 2, 1942, a Spitfire pilot was forced to bale out over the English Channel landing in the sea four miles off the French coast on the edge of a minefield. His leader orbited overhead the dinghy and transmitted an emergency call. The naval authorities at Dover considered it to be impossible to get a launch through the minefield. They also considered it too dangerous for a Walrus amphibian to make an attempt. Despite this advice, Fletcher immediately volunteered to make a rescue attempt and took off with a Spitfire squadron providing an escort.

"He arrived on the scene as another Spitfire squadron engaged enemy fighters trying to interfere with the rescue. He located the dinghy and landed 150 yards away and taxied towards the survivor who failed to grasp the boathook on the first pass as he fell out of his dinghy. In the strong wind and choppy sea, Fletcher made another attempt when the pilot was hauled on board. He then taxied clear of the minefield and took off, just clearing a floating mine. Throughout the rescue, the Walrus had come under heavy fire from shore batteries.

"The Air Officer Commanding of No. 11 (Fighter) Group strongly recommended Fletcher for the award of the Victoria Cross. He wrote 'Sergeant Fletcher was fully aware of the risks involved when he volunteered for the task. He carried out the rescue with conspicuous gallantry … he ignored all dangers and through coolness, considered judgement and skill, succeeded in picking up the fighter pilot'.

"In the event, Fletcher was awarded an immediate DFM, the next highest gallantry award available for a SNCO at that time."

Tom Fletcher was soon awarded a bar to the DFM and later an immediate DFC. The latter award came after a day on which he had picked up a bomber crew and then landed in rough seas to save a Typhoon pilot. In the conditions he could not take off again and began to taxi the Walrus across the channel. The aircraft eventually sank and those on board were picked up by a Royal Navy launch.

His other exploits included the rescue of a Canadian fighter pilot in 1944, who had come down close to the French coast. To effect the rescue Fletcher had to fly over enemy territory and through heavy anti-aircraft fire which wounded his crewman. Nonetheless, the Canadian was picked up and returned to England.

T

Torbeau – See Bristol Beaufighter.

U

U-boat – German submarine. From the German word "Unterseeboot".

V

Vickers Vildebeest – The first operational example of this large biplane torpedo-bomber came to Donibristle on the Firth of Forth in 1932 for No. 100 Squadron. This followed several years of gestation and difficulties. Vildebeests were still in service at the outbreak of war and some flew against the Japanese from Singapore. A second operator of the Wildebeest was the RNZAF.

Vickers Warwick – Seen as a development of the Wellington for service in Bomber Command, the Warwick was considerably delayed by problems with the Rolls Royce Vulture engine. One prototype flew in August 1939, powered by two of these, but a switch was made to

Vickers Warwick ASR Mk.I, HF 944 K, of Coastal Command's No. 282 Squadron, based at St Eval, in flight, carrying the short Mk.IA lifeboat.

the Bristol Centaurus. Then there was a shortage of those engines and the Pratt & Whitney Double Wasp became the third powerplant to be associated with the Warwick.

Development had dragged to the point where the type had been overtaken by the entry into Bomber Command service of the various four-engine "heavies". At the start of 1943 it was decided that the best could be made of the situation by converting the Warwick to be used for air sea rescue. In this guise it would carry a lifeboat beneath the fuselage. Accordingly, the Warwick ASR.I entered service in August 1943 with No. 280 Squadron as it moved from Thorney Island to Thornaby. The squadron retained the Warwick, through transfers and detachments (including service at Strubby, Langham, Beccles, St Eval, Aldergrove, Lossiemouth and Reykjavik) until it was disbanded in June 1946.

The design was gradually developed in various ways for Coastal Command. Bristol Centaurus engines were fitted to the GR.II general reconnaissance variant. Both Transport Command and BOAC operated a transport version.

Vickers Wellington – A twin-engine medium bomber that, when it first flew in 1936, was seen as well in advance of existing types and was a key contributor to Bomber Command's operations in the early years of the war. It was particularly noted for its "geodetic" construction (designed by Barnes Wallis and already utilised in the Vickers Wellesley), using a criss-crossing metal mesh, intended to add greatly to the strength of the fuselage.

The Wellington B Mk III, very active in Bomber Command from 1941, was considered by some to be a great improvement on what had gone before. One pilot who brought a badly damaged Mk III back from Germany, despite his own serious wounds, commented that he would not have achieved the feat if he had not been flying a Mk III.

In Coastal Command service Wellingtons added to the variety of aircraft used in the anti-submarine offensive.

See also entry for De-Gaussing.

Victoria Cross – The Crimean War, which broke out in 1853, served to highlight the lack of British awards for gallant service in action. The most important outcome of the discussion generated was the institution of the Victoria Cross, which ever since has been the highest British decoration for valour. The warrant for the VC was signed by Queen Victoria on January 29 1856.

The VC warrant has been revised many times over the years, the Air Force being mentioned for the first time in the warrant of May 22 1920, which included amongst those eligible for the award, "Officers, Warrant Officers, Non Commissioned Officers and airmen in the ranks of Our Air Force, or the Air Forces of our Dominions, Colonies, Dependencies or Protectorates."

The first award of the VC to an airman was announced in *The London Gazette* on May 22 1915. The decoration went posthumously to Lieutenant William Barnard "Will" Rhodes-Moorhouse, No. 2 Squadron, Royal Flying Corps, who was terribly wounded while attacking a railway line at Courtrai in France, during the first Battle of Ypres. He regained British lines and managed to make his report, but eventually died from his wounds.

During the Second World War four pilots serving with Coastal Command received the VC. In order of the awards being earned they were:

Flying Officer Kenneth Campbell (Posthumous Award)
On April 6 1941, Ken Campbell was the skipper of a Beaufort of No. 22 Squadron, one of six detailed to fly from St Eval in Cornwall to attack the German battle cruiser *Gneisenau*. The ship was moored in

the harbour at the French port of Brest in Brittany and was protected by a vast assembly of anti-aircraft guns. Campbell initially achieved surprise and released his torpedo from a height of 50 feet. The aircraft was then hit by a concentrated barrage of fire and crashed into the harbour, with no survivors. The torpedo from the doomed Beaufort struck the *Gneisenau* and caused considerable damage.

Ken Campbell was 23 years old and had attended Sedbergh School before reading natural sciences at Clare College, Cambridge. His crew consisted of Sergeant Scott, DFM, RCAF, navigator, Sergeant Mulliss, wireless operator and Flight Sergeant Hillman, air gunner. Hillman had been attached to No. 235 Squadron during August 1940 and, as a result, qualified for the Battle of Britain Clasp.

From the Clare College website and marking the 70th anniversary of Campbell's VC action was the following dedication:

The Master, Professor Tony Badger, commented: "Kenneth Campbell was one of 152 Clare men who gave their lives for their country in World War II. He was one of only two Clare men to be awarded the VC. So many of the generation of Clare men admitted by Sir Henry Thirkill in the 1930s went on to have very distinguished and worthwhile careers in business, the professions and public service after 1945. That they were able to do so was the result of the sacrifices made by young fliers like Kenneth Campbell. When I look at today's graduating class, it is very humbling to think that someone seventy years before, less than two years after his own graduation, was dying for our country and for the freedoms which we all take for granted. I shall remind this summer's granduands [those about to graduate] of that sacrifice at this summer's graduation ceremonies."

Flying Officer Lloyd Allan Trigg, DFC, RNZAF (Posthumous Award)
Lloyd Trigg was serving with No. 200 Squadron, based at Yundum in The Gambia, West Africa. The squadron was converting from Hudsons to Liberators when, on August 11 1943, Trigg took off

from Bathurst (now Banjul) on a shipping patrol, which was his first sortie in a Liberator. About 240 miles south west of Dakar, a surfaced U-boat, *U-468*, was sighted. The Liberator launched an attack and was hit and set ablaze by fire from its target. Nonetheless the attack was pressed home and a number of depth charges were released over the submarine, which sank in a few minutes. The blazing Liberator crashed nearby and all on board were killed.

There were seven survivors from the crew of the U-boat. Among them were the commander, Oberleutnant zur See Clemens Schmong and the first lieutenant, Leutnant zur See Alfons Heimannsberg. Their accounts of what had happened led to the award of the VC to Lloyd Trigg.

In 1998 Trigg's VC was sold at auction by Spink for £155,000, then a world record auction price for a VC. "Tall (5 ft 10 in), sporting a small but neat moustache, Trigg said very little and remained reserved, seldom visiting the mess except for necessities. A fellow pilot summed up Trigg by saying, 'He seldom spoke but had a fantastic determination. He hated the Germans and his sole interest was in getting the war won so that he could return to his family.'" (From *For Valour* by Chaz Bowyer).

Flight Lieutenant David Ernest Hornell, RCAF (*Posthumous Award*)
David Hornell volunteered for the RCAF, aged 30, at the beginning of 1941. After training as a pilot, he served in Canada. In October 1943 he was posted to No. 106 Squadron, RCAF, based at Dartmouth, Nova Scotia, with Consolidated Canso aircraft, a name used by the Canadian Air Force for the type known in the RAF as the Catalina. The squadron quickly moved to Reykjavik, Iceland. From May 1944, a detachment was maintained at Wick in the north of Scotland, with crews moving between Iceland and Scotland on a regular basis.

On June 24, Hornell and his crew were almost ten hours into a patrol from Wick, when a surfaced submarine (*U-1225*) was seen and an attack was made. Although the Canso was hit repeatedly and set on fire, depth charges were dropped accurately, causing the U-boat to sink. Despite one engine falling off, Flight Lieutenant Hornell managed to ditch and all eight crew members escaped. However, one dinghy soon deflated. Hornell had removed his trousers as he sought to reach a man struggling in the sea; he then used the trousers to bail water from the surviving dinghy. High winds and a heavy swell created more problems.

A Catalina returning from patrol saw a distress cartridge and located the Canso crew and survivors from the U-boat. It requested help and circled the Canadians for fourteen hours. After sixteen hours a Warwick arrived and dropped a lifeboat, but it landed hundreds of yards from the dinghy. Hornell, by this time blind and very weak, attempted to swim to retrieve it, but one of his comrades held on to him. Eventually a Sunderland directed a rescue launch to the spot. By this time two of the crew had died and David Hornell died shortly after being taken on board. His body and the living members of his crew were taken to Lerwick, Shetland.

In addition to the VC awarded to David Hornell, Flying Officer Demoney, the second pilot, received the DSO, Flying Officer Matheson (navigator) and Flying Officer Campbell (wireless operator/ air gunner) were awarded DFCs and there were DFMs for Flight Sergeants Bodnoff and Cole, both wireless operator/air gunners. The two flight engineers who had perished, Sergeants Scott and St Laurent, were Mentioned in Despatches.

The Victoria Cross was presented to David Hornell's widow, Genevieve, by the Earl of Athlone, Governor General of Canada.

Flying Officer John Alexander Cruickshank
John Cruickshank, born in Aberdeen, served as a Territorial in the Royal Artillery and was called up on the outbreak of war. He transferred to the RAF and undertook pilot training in Canada and the USA. From March 1943, he flew Catalinas with No. 210 Squadron. He completed

Flying Officer John
Cruickshank, VC.

almost fifty operational patrols and, on July 17 1944 set off for yet another from Sullom Voe, Shetland. The ten-man crew of the "boat" included a new pilot gaining experience and a rigger.

West of the Lofoten Islands, a vessel was detected by radar. This proved to be a U-boat proceeding on the surface. "Jock" Cruickshank mounted an attack, but the Catalina's depth charges failed to release and he went round again. This time the aircraft was hit badly by fire from the U-boat. Flying Officer Dickson, the navigator, was killed and it would later be discovered that the skipper had received more than seventy wounds, though he did not tell anyone. He released the depth charges himself, causing the U-boat to sink.

The U-boat under attack during Cruickshank's VC action.

Flight Sergeant Garnett, the second pilot, took over the controls and set course for base. Cruickshank fainted from loss of blood and was carried to a bunk. Flight Sergeant Appleton, one of the wireless operator/air gunners, started to dress the skipper's wounds, discovering more as he proceeded. Appleton restrained Cruickshank when he came to and tried to go forward. Cruickshank refused morphine in case it inhibited his ability to fly and command, but frequently lost consciousness.

Over Sullom Voe Cruickshank insisted on being helped forward. He was placed in the second pilot's seat and ordered that the aircraft circle until daylight. Then Cruickshank and Garnett between them landed and drove the Catalina on to the beach.

"In August 1944, a stricken Catalina flying boat ran up on the beach at Sullom Voe, Coastal Command's base in the Shetland Islands, where O'Connor was station medical officer. As he boarded the aircraft, he immediately realised that only a blood transfusion on the spot would give its pilot, Cruickshank, any chance of survival. Using such limited equipment as he had available, including a chamber pot, O'Connor stabilised the wounded man sufficiently to move him to hospital." (From the *Daily Telegraph* obituary of Air Vice-Marshal Patrick O'Connor, April 10 2001).

As well as the VC awarded to Jock Cruickshank, Jack Garnett received the DFM. In 2016 John Cruickshank was the only living recipient of the VC from the Second World War.

West Africa – Coastal Command operated from various West African bases, from 1941, in the war against U-boats.

"The ground staff encountered most of the initial difficulties owing to the problem of supply. Much that was required for servicing the

Maintenance work in West Africa.

flying boats was delayed in arrival. But a substitute was found locally for everything. It was found, for instance that homemade groundnut oil worked splendidly in the hydraulics, and that a packing box nail could be converted into a usable split pin. Oil pipeline joints were packed with sheets of brown paper, and toilet paper was used as oil filters. Nine thicknesses of this paper, the ground engineers discovered, made a fine impromptu oil filter." (From *Coastal Command at War* by Squadron Leader Tom Dudley Gordon).

Western Approaches – The area of the Atlantic Ocean immediately to the west of the British Isles and going west towards Iceland. Much shipping passed through the Approaches to reach Britain, the estuaries of the Clyde and the Mersey in particular, and it was therefore a major hunting ground for U-boats and a major area of activity for Coastal Command. In the Royal Navy, Commander in Chief, Western Approaches, was based in Liverpool from February 1941. No. 15 Group, Coastal Command, also established its HQ there, having previously been at Plymouth. Co-operation between the Navy and the airmen proved especially productive in Liverpool.

Part of Derby House, the former headquarters of Western Approaches Command, is now the Western Approaches – Liverpool Museum.

In April 2013 a memorial, provided by Anglesey Council and the Royal Navy, was unveiled to Admiral Sir Max Kennedy Horton, who was Commander in Chief Western Approaches Command from November 1942. The memorial is situated in the library in the village of Rhosneigr, where he was born.

The BBC quoted historian Charles McCain as commenting on the high circles in which Sir Max moved, but also saying, "But his background? Parents [his father was a failed stockbroker]? His childhood? The source of his inner strength? His heroes? His inner life? Of Sir Max as a man? We have no idea.

"We do know this: the men and women under his command in Western Approaches never came to love him. They never came to like him. But they came quickly to respect him and even more, have the greatest confidence in him – for Sir Max radiated confidence."

South Western Approaches and North Western Approaches were Allied terms, depending on the geographical area involved.

W

White Crow – Description for Coastal Command aircraft painted white, after the work of the Operational Research Unit (see separate entry) demonstrated that, in northern latitudes, with average conditions of sky and cloud, plain white paint, covering the sides and under surfaces of an aircraft, reduced considerably the visibility of that aircraft when viewed from the surface of the sea.

From the summer of 1941 this paint scheme was applied to many aircraft operating against U-boats.

Women's Auxiliary Air Force – The WAAF was established in June 1939, so that men could be released for operational roles. A Women's Royal Air Force had served for a time at the end of the Great War. This name was used again from 1949, when the WAAF was re-formed and, in 1994, the women's service became fully integrated into the RAF.

There was much initial opposition to the concept of women serving in roles where they might come under fire or (in control rooms for example) hear radio broadcasts which, in the stress of the moment, could contain foul language or the sound of men trapped in burning aircraft.

WAAFs quickly proved the doubters wrong. During 1940 a number of WAAFs earned gallantry awards, three of which went to personnel serving at the Coastal Command station at Detling in Kent.

In the early hours of May 31 1940, Corporal Daphne Pearson, a twenty-nine-year-old medical attendant, was one of the first people to

WAAFs load crew kit into a Coastal Command aircraft.

react when an Avro Anson of No. 500 Squadron crashed at Detling and caught fire. The aircraft had been detailed to attack enemy shipping off Boulogne, but still had bombs on board.

Corporal Pearson dragged clear the badly injured skipper of the Anson, Pilot Officer David Bond, and shielded him from explosions, covering his head with her tin hat. Two other members of the crew had got clear, but one was unaccounted for and, with explosions continuing, Daphne Pearson went back into the wreckage to try to find him. He was in fact dead.

Once Pilot Officer Bond had been removed by ambulance, Corporal Pearson went to help the medical officer. At 08.00 hours she returned to duty as usual.

The award of the Empire Gallantry Medal to Daphne Pearson, by now commissioned, was announced on July 19 1940. Shortly afterwards the George Cross was established and it was decided that living recipients of the EGM would exchange their medals for the GC, as well as next of kin of recipients who had died since September 3 1939.

Parachute packing.

Another form of recognition that came to Daphne Pearson was that she was painted by the eminent artist, Dame Laura Knight. The depiction, as planned, seems to have caused a stir. Daphne Pearson wrote to her mother:

"I am being painted in a tin helmet and holding a rifle – Air Min [Air Ministry] will be furious but Dame Laura says my helmet is rather like a bonnet on the back of my head and the rifle makes a good line – WAAFs are 'not to carry arms' – controversy is still raging and this will upset the apple cart. Dame Laura is adamant and firm."

In the final painting the rifle had become a respirator. Whether Dame Laura changed her mind by herself, or was leaned on by authority appears not to be clear.

Daphne Pearson GC was demobilised in 1946. She emigrated to Australia in 1959 and died in 2000. She was an active member of the Victoria Cross and George Cross Association.

David Bond survived the war and founded the Bond helicopter business. He died in 1977. Members of his family were present in 2010 when a plaque commemorating Daphne Pearson was unveiled at Detling.

Bibliography

The National Archives
AIR 20
AIR 27.
AIR 28
WO 98

Published Books
Alexander, Kristen, *Jack Davenport, Beaufighter Leader* (Allen & Unwin, 2009).

Anon., *A Brief History of the Royal Air Force* (HMSO, 2004).

Anon., *Coastal Command* (HMSO, 1942).

Anon., *We Speak from the Air*, (HMSO, 1942).

Ashworth, Chris, *RAF Coastal Command, 1936-1969* (Patrick Stephens, 1992).

Baff, Flight Lieutenant K.C., *Maritime is Number Ten* (Netley, 1983).

Barker, Ralph, *Ship Busters!* (Grub Street, 2009 edition).

Bird, Andrew D., *A Separate Little War* (Grub Street, 2008).

Bird, Andrew D., *Coastal Dawn* (Grub Street, 2012).

Bowyer, Chaz., *For Valour* (Grub Street, 1992).

Bowyer, Chaz., *Men of Coastal Command 1939-1945* (William Kimber, 1985).

Carter, Ian, *Coastal Command 1939-1945* (Ian Allan Publishing, 2004).

Churchill, Winston, *The Second World War, Vol II, Their Finest Hour* (Cassell & Co, 1949).

Colston Shepherd, E., *The Air Force of To-day* (Blackie & Son, 1939).

Conyers Nesbit, Roy, *The Strike Wings* (HMSO edition, 1995).

Crook, M. J., *The Evolution of the Victoria Cross* (Midas Books, in association with The Ogilby Trust, 1975).

Crosby, Francis, *The World Encyclopedia of Bombers* (Anness Publishing, 2010).

De Groot, Gerard J., *Liberal Crusader* (Hurst & Company, 1993).

Donitz, Karl, *Memoirs*, (Da Capo Press, 1997).

Douglas, Sholto, with Wright, Robert, *Years of Command* (Collins, 1966).

Downing, Taylor, *Spies in the Sky* (Little, Brown, 2011).

Dudley Gordon, Squadron Leader Tom, *Coastal Command at War* (Jarrolds, 1943).

Edwards, Gron, *Norwegian Patrol* (Airlife, 1985).

Foxley-Norris, Christopher, *A Lighter Shade of Blue* (Ian Allan, 1978).

Harris, Marshal of the Royal Air Force Sir Arthur, *Bomber Offensive* (Collins, 1947).

Hendrie, Andrew, *The Cinderella Service* (Pen and Sword Aviation, 2006).

Hunt, Leslie, *Twenty-one Squadrons* (Crecy Books, 1992).

Jenkins, Roy, *Churchill* (Macmillan, 2001).

Joubert de la Ferte, Air Chief Marshal Sir Philip, KCB, CMG, DSO, *The Third Service* (Thames and Hudson, 1955).

Liddell Hart, Basil, *The Defence of Britain* (Faber & Faber, 1939).

Mondey, David, *American Aircraft of World War II* (Chancellor Press, 1996).

Mondey, David, *British Aircraft of World War II* (Hamlyn Publishing Group, 1982).

Moulard, Geneviève, *Les Femmes de la Royal Air Force 1918-1945* (Marines Editions, 2012).

Niestle, Axel, *German U-boat Losses During World War II* (Greenhill Books, 1998).

Pollard, Captain A. O., VC, MC, DCM, *Leaders of Britain in the Royal Air Force* (Hutchinson & Co, 1940).

Probert, Henry, *Bomber Harris, His Life and Times* (Greenhill Books, 2003).

Probert, Air Commodore Henry, *High Commanders of the RAF* (HMSO, 1991).

Richards, D. and Saunders H., *The Royal Air Force 1939-1945* (HMSO, 1974).

Roe, F. Gordon, *The Bronze Cross* (P. R. Gawthorn, 1945).

Sharpe, Peter, *U-boat Fact File* (Midland Publishing, 1998).

Stanley, Peter. *Air Battle Europe, 1939-1945* (Time-Life Books [Australia], 1987).

Taylor, Les, *Banff Strike Wing* (Halsgrove, 2010).

Terraine, John, *The Right of the Line* (Wordsworth Editions edition, 1997).

Tilley, John, *Churchill's Favourite Socialist* (Holyoake Books, 1995).

Wynn, Kenneth G., *Men of the Battle of Britain* Third edition (Frontline Books in association with Battle of Britain Memorial Trust, 2015).

Wynn, Kenneth G., *U-boat Operations of the Second World War* (Naval Institute Press, two volumes, 1998).

Internet sources

Awm.gov.au

Catalina.org.uk

Channeldash.org

CWGC.org

Gov.uk

Handard.parliament.uk

Historyofwar.org

Militaryhsitoryonline.com

Norfolk-on-line.co.uk

Pembrokedock.org

Rafbnmp.org.uk
Raf.mod.uk
Royalnavy.mod.uk
Sunderlandtrust.org.uk
Trinityhouse.co.uk
Uboat.net

Periodicals
Britain at War Magazine
Daily Telegraph
Coastal Command Review
Evening Standard
Glasgow Herald
Insider (Spink & Son house magazine)
Journal of The Victoria Cross Society
London Gazette
RAF Historical Society Journal
The Times
The War Illustrated
Western Telegraph